W9-AQX-021

Teaching the Helping Skills

A FIELD INSTRUCTOR'S GUIDE

SECOND EDITION

Lawrence Shulman

**COUNCIL
ON SOCIAL WORK EDUCATION**

*To Alex Gitterman, my good friend and colleague. For all the years
of his wisdom, courage, and humor, I am forever grateful.*

Library of Congress Cataloging-in-Publication Data

Shulman, Lawrence.
    Teaching the helping skills : a field instructor's guide /
Lawrence Shulman.—2nd ed.
       p.   cm.
    Includes bibliographical references.
    ISBN 0-87293-036-X (pbk.)
    1. Social service—Field work—Study and education.   2. Social
work education.   I. Title.
HV11.S494   1993
361'.0071—dc20   93-10698
                                                                          CIP

Manufactured in the United States of America

Cover design by Naylor Design, Inc., Bryantown, MD

CONTENTS

FOREWORD

In 1988, as a part of its strategic planning process, the Council on Social Work Education (CSWE) conducted several focus group meetings with members throughout the country. In response to the question of what CSWE could do to be of more service to members, we most frequently heard the request, help us learn to do our jobs better—to become better educators. We have attempted to respond in several ways: through greater focus on knowledge and skill development in faculty development institutes and sessions at the annual program meeting; through the production of satellite videocasts; and through publication of targeted reports and monographs.

With the publication of the second edition of *Teaching the Helping Skills: A Field Instructor's Guide*, CSWE makes an addition to this response by providing another important tool to improve social work education. Though brief, this monograph serves as a powerful guide for field instructors and supervisors to enhance their teaching of core practice skills. Its power is derived from the sources Shulman has used in developing it: interactional theory, empirical research, and years of hands-on experience as teacher and trainer. In this regard, the guide itself presents a model for knowledge and skill development.

By emphasizing the mediation role that the supervisor plays between the student and what is to be learned, Shulman challenges the supervisor to master not only the content of the subject matter but also the interactional process by which it is conveyed. Thus, an essential element of supervision is "modeling" the skills that are being taught in the supervisory interactions with the student. A key concept is that of *parallelism*—that is, the student learns such skills as contracting, tuning-in, empathy, confrontation, dealing with authority, and so forth, as much by his or her interacting with the supervisor as by examining his or her own practice with clients. How this is accomplished is demonstrated in numerous case examples.

A major addition to this edition is the systematic inclusion of content on teaching practice with diverse populations. Shulman stresses the importance of the supervisor modeling, in his or her relationship with the student, the dynamics and skills involved in working with diverse populations. The discussion and case examples demonstrate the importance of cutting through the natural resistance to confront feelings and attitudes that are generally taboo in our society and that create subtle (and sometime not-so-subtle) barriers to the helping process.

As almost every social work student will testify, field instruction is the primary element in learning beginning practice skills. For both student and instructor, it is an intense, complicated, and highly demanding process. This guide provides a valuable tool to ease that process and helps integrate the field experience into the rest of the curriculum.

Donald W. Beless, PhD
Executive Director

INTRODUCTION

The second edition of this guide draws upon three of the author's texts: *Interactional Supervision* (Shulman, 1993); *The Skills of Helping Individuals, Families and Groups* (3rd ed.) (Shulman, 1992); and *Interactional Social Work Practice: Toward an Empirical Theory* (Shulman, 1991). It is designed to help field instructors to integrate class and field teaching of practice skills. It includes a description of the interactional paradigm that has guided the development of the author's practice, supervision, and teaching frameworks. Although the interactional approach provides the integrating framework for the text, many of the practice and supervision skills described can be useful for field instructors using other theoretical models.

To explore the educational function of field instruction, this guide first sets out some underlying assumptions about the teaching-learning process. It then summarizes a number of the constructs of the interactional paradigm, including an oppression psychology model for understanding the adaptive efforts of a range of oppressed and vulnerable populations (e.g., persons of color, survivors of sexual abuse, and persons with physical and mental impairments). Finally, it examines how the teaching function is implemented in field instruction.

The main part of the work is a section on teaching core practice skills for practice with clients. Each skill is illustrated with process recording excerpts from student practice with clients. Methods that supervisors can use to help students develop the skill are then discussed and illustrated with process recording excerpts from supervision practice. This approach highlights the parallel process in which supervisors, in implementing their teaching role, model the same interactional skills that students need in their work with clients. This edition also explores issues of diversity and the need for cultural-practice sensitivity as these skills are adapted to different racial and ethnic populations. Findings from the author's recent research on social work practice and on supervision—on which the empirical foundations of this interactional model have been built—are also included.

Appendix A provides examples of written exercises that students can use in assessing their practice skills, working relationship with clients, sources of social support, as well as client strengths. Appendix B provides a standard for skill development for beginners in the field that supervisors can use to evaluate their own students' progress.

The focus in this guide is on interactional skills: These skills represent only a part of the total learning curriculum the student requires. Field instruction includes work on human growth and behavior theory, assessment skills, knowledge about population groups and specific problems and about research findings of importance to social work practice, job management skills, and other such areas. Even highly skilled supervisors may find it difficult to articulate what it is they do with clients and to develop techniques for imparting their views on method. Many supervisors experience this area as threatening and often prefer instead to discuss the client, values, or the underlying knowledge base. These discussions are indeed important, but when they become a substitute for dealing with specific skill development, an important gap is left in the educational process. Thus, because interactional skills are both least often addressed in the literature and most likely to cause supervisors difficulty, they are given special attention.

UNDERLYING ASSUMPTIONS ABOUT TEACHING AND LEARNING

The teaching and learning process in supervision has been profoundly affected by acceptance of the myth that teaching essentially involves transmitting existing ideas to learners who somehow absorb and adopt them. This myth suggests that all that is necessary for teaching is to have a good grasp of the knowledge and to be able to transmit it clearly, by organizing ideas well, articulating them systematically, and then illustrating them.

As with most myths, there is an element of truth in this one. A study of university-level teaching (Shulman, 1972) found that these two skills—having knowledge and the ability to transmit it—were associated most highly with effective instruction. The next most important variable, however, was the instructor's ability to empathize with students, and the fourth was the ability to present ideas so that they are open to challenge. These findings suggest that there may be more to teaching than just knowing a subject and presenting it to students. In fact, they support what we usually experience as consumers of teaching: we have had teachers who were very knowledgeable and clear presenters from whom we learned very little, and others who were less certain of their grasp of the subject and more hesitant in their presentation from whom we yet learned a great deal.

In short, experience should suggest that the teaching and learning process is a complex one, which is affected by many factors related to the subject area, the context of learning, the specific qualities of the teacher and the learner, and the interaction between the two individuals. The learner is not simply a passive object onto which the teacher can project already developed ideas. Rather, the learner is actively involved in the learning process. This view, proposed by William James and elaborated by John Dewey, maintains that "the organism is not simply receiving impressions and then answering them. The organism is doing something, it is actively seeking and selecting certain stimuli" (Dewey, 1916, p. 46).

In discussing education in the classroom, William Schwartz (1979) also commented on the importance of the active involvement of the learner. Citing the contribution of the 18th-century historian and philosopher, Giambiattista Vico, Schwartz argued that "this is the true process by which students learn: they cannot own their knowledge until they have 'made' it, worked it over, put their mark on the data, imposed their own order upon it, and altered it to fit with what they already have" (p. 19).

This is the central assumption of this work on the educational function of supervision. The students are active participants in the learning process, and the supervisor's job is as much to present ideas as to monitor the ways in which the students relate to these ideas. This may range from simply monitoring students' eyes to ensuring they are following directions for filling out a complex form, to empathizing with students while trying to help them tackle a difficult practice issue.

It can also include discerning the subtle interplay that takes place between the supervisor and the student that has been described as the *authority theme* (Shulman, 1992); the feelings for both parties resulting from this relationship can enhance the learning or generate major obstacles to the integration of new ideas.

Knowing the subject and clearly transmitting the concepts is an important pre-condition to teaching, but these skills should not be confused with the entire process. Schwartz (1979) put it nicely:

> In this light, the problem of the transmitting function is not that it is "unprogressive" or even unproductive, but simply that it does not go far enough into the educational process. When the facts are told, the notes taken down, the "truth" laid out, the work is only just begun. The hardest part remains. (p. 19)

The following section discusses some of the requirements for effective teaching and learning, and identifies some of the obstacles that can frustrate the endeavor.

Requirements for Effective Learning

A first requirement for effective learning is that the learner must have a stake in the outcome. A student who is to learn new skills or procedures must be willing to invest some affect, or feeling, in the process. This will only take place when, as Dewey put it, the learner is allowed to "share in the social use to which his action is put" (p. 44). In effect, he suggests that students should become copartners with supervisors, so that by engaging in the activity together, they can have the same interest in its accomplishment and share in the ideas and emotions that result.

This may seem rather obvious, but its implications for teaching are often ignored. The supervisor must be clear about the usefulness of the content for the student; otherwise, the connection will not be made. For example, an orientation program with extensive content on the structure of the organization or its policies may have little meaning in the day-to-day practice of a student. The orientation becomes an illusion of work in which limited real learning occurs.

In many situations, the connection between the content to be learned and the student's present sense of urgency may be only partial or difficult to perceive without extensive experience. Then, beginning supervisory efforts must search out this connection and help the student understand clearly why the information is important, before the ideas are presented. This is a form of contracting at the start of a supervision session; the supervisor concentrates on helping the student to find the connection between the subject matter to be learned and the student's felt needs.

A second requirement for effective learning is that the student must be actively involved in the investigation of ideas, building his or her own models of reality. No matter how much the supervisor may want to impart understanding to a student or to share quickly the results of her or his own years or learning, it cannot be done. John Holt (1969) put it well:

> We teachers—perhaps all human beings—are in the grip of an astonishing delusion. We think that we can take a picture, a structure, a working model of something, constructed in our own minds out of long experience and familiarity, and by turning that model into a string of words, transplant it whole into the mind of someone else. (p. 39)

Many teachers seem to persist in believing that by uttering the words they can transmit an idea (even though their own educational experience has taught them differently). If we think back to how we learned something new, we know that the ideas did not exist until we created them for ourselves. *Real learning requires the active construction of knowledge by the learner, using all the resources available. The teacher can be one main resource among others, but the construction of the idea, fact, or theory, and so on, must be undertaken by the learner.*

Complete comprehension of the idea that knowledge does not exist for the learner until he or she re-creates it leads to major changes in thinking about the teaching-learning process. *Teaching cannot be conceived of as simply handing over knowledge or covering the agenda. Instead, the teacher must concentrate on the interaction between the learner and the ideas to be learned, placing a priority on the continuous monitoring of the learning interaction, and keeping in touch with the learner's progress in constructing the ideas.*

This emphasis is especially important in teaching complex skills that may have taken years to develop. Supervisors are apt to forget the steps they followed to deepen their own understanding of the content. Ideas that have become rather obvious to them may not be the least bit simple, or obvious, to their students. For example, learning to contract with clients—by clarifying purpose and role and by reaching for client feedback—may seem an obvious process to supervisors. However, as workers or students, they may have had to struggle to develop ways of doing this quickly. Perhaps, they thought they understood the idea of contracting in the first semester, only to discover in the second semester, as they got bogged down in the work phase, they had no more than a superficial understanding of the importance of the idea. As they moved to a new setting, changed their practicum, or started practice with a different category of clients or using a new modality such as group or family work, each new situation helped to deepen their grasp of the contracting notion.

Unless supervisors work hard at it, they can forget about how they had to construct, bit by bit, their understanding of an idea such as contracting. They think they can simply hand over the years of learning and are surprised to discover that students are having great difficulty constructing even a simple version of the idea. As learners who themselves have ventured into this subject area, who have discovered some of the shortcuts and are only now aware of some of the pitfalls, supervisors can guide their students and make their trips more direct. Supervisors, however, cannot take the trip for their students.

Another requirement for effective learning is that the learner must have structured opportunities for using the information presented. A theory about social behavior, for example, will become meaningful when a student employs the principles in order to understand a "real"client. The doing part, the application of theory, strengthens the student's understanding of its content. Thus, knowing and doing are closely related.

Practice skill development is another area where this is most obvious. Students being taught a new skill are more likely to learn it if they can practice it while it is being taught. For example, students developing group leadership skills can only go so far in their understanding before they will be blocked in their learning by a lack of practical experience. When actual practice experiences are not easily available, laboratory simulations may be useful, but they lack the reality of trying skills out with real clients.

In summary, the three essential requirements for effective learning are that the learner (1) perceive an investment in the knowledge, (2) be actively involved in creating the ideas, and (3) have an opportunity to practice the use of the information. Even with these elements present, many obstacles can emerge to block the learning effort. The supervisor helps overcome these obstacles through attention to the teaching-learning process as the student develops mastery of the skills needed for effective work.

THE INTERACTIONAL FRAMEWORK FOR SUPERVISION AND PRACTICE

Before describing the *interactional model*, the diversity of theories guiding the helping professions should be noted. The social work profession has only just begun to use theories to guide empirical research into practice. Because we are still just beginning this crucial theory-building process, there is room in the profession for a range of views—and this is a healthy state.

All practitioners eventually develop their own practice frameworks. Some frameworks are more, and others less, explicit. Workers judge them by how well they work in explaining their practice. The framework for social work described in this guide has been most helpful to the author in his practice, his theory building, and his research. It is not dogmatically engraved in stone, however, and will continue to be used as a framework just as long as it appears to do the job. Readers should test its ideas against their own sense of reality and use those portions that seem helpful. Many of the skills and intermediate models are not bound by one approach and can easily fit into other theoretical frameworks.

The Interactional Theory

At the core of the interactional theory of social work practice is a model of the helping process in which the skill of the worker helps to create a positive working relationship. In turn, this relationship is the medium through which the worker influences the outcome of practice. This simple model can be visualized as follows:

WORKER SKILL $\longleftrightarrow$ RELATIONSHIP $\longleftrightarrow$ OUTCOMES OF PRACTICE

Another model incorporated into this theory has to do with the relationship between our clients' ability to manage their *feelings* and their ability to manage their *problems*. These ideas were developed as part of the theory-building effort described in other books by the author (Shulman, 1991, 1992). The construct is based on the assumption that how we feel has a powerful effect on how we act. The relationship between feelings and action is reciprocal in nature, as how we act impacts on how we feel. This model fits well with an oppression psychology model such as the one developed by the West Indian–born psychiatrist Frantz Fanon (Bulhan, 1988). While Fanon was most concerned with the "psycho-affective injuries" experienced by slaves and colonized communities of color, many of his concepts generalize well to other generally oppressed populations such as people with mental and physical impairments, and clients who have experienced oppression related to gender, race, class, sexual orientation, and so forth.

To illustrate these core concepts, the author will use the example of survivors of sexual abuse. It is not uncommon for female survivors of childhood sexual abuse to describe themselves as feeling like "damaged goods" as they enter their teenage years. These clients often respond to the oppression they have experienced by internalizing a negative self-image and by assuming some form of responsibility for what was done to them. They may express feelings of guilt and concern that they may have been seductive toward the offending adult. This is what the oppression psychology of Fanon would have described as the pattern in which a survivor of long-term oppression internalizes the "external oppressor."

Oppression psychology suggests that long-term oppression leads to many forms of alienation and psycho-affective injuries. Defensive maneuvers are necessary for survival, although they often are maladaptive in the long run. For example, with the survivor of sexual abuse, symptoms of depression and personal apathy often cover an underlying rage that had been suppressed in order to survive. The use of alcohol and drugs provides an escape, a flight from the pain associated with the abuse; it is an example of the self-destructive behavior often evidenced by oppressed clients who become, in Fanon's terms, *autopressors*. The phenomenon of using fight or flight as a defense against pain has been a commonly observed pattern with individuals, families, groups, and even entire communities.

The impact of low self-image may lead these teenage survivors to enter into relationships and life patterns that tend to perpetuate their exploitation. For example, a low sense of self-esteem may lead to relationships with exploitive partners who use physical, emotional, or sexual violence to maintain control over the life of the survivor. The use of drugs and involvement in the street culture may lead to prostitution. The client's actions, related to the client's feelings, may in turn deepen the sense of being damaged. Thus, a negative, reciprocal relationship between how the client feels and how the client acts results in a deepening of the problems in living.

An intervention is needed to disrupt this vicious cycle. In the example of the survivor, as the worker helps the client (or group of clients) to examine the underlying pain and rage in her life, and to face the *oppressor within*, the client can begin to take control of the emotions and more effectively manage them, instead of the client being managed by the emotions. In general, the principle of dealing with feelings in pursuit of purpose will cause the worker to help clients to connect their feelings with their actions. As these feelings are better managed by clients, they can begin to more effectively manage their life problems. For example, the teenage survivor in this illustration may begin to modify self-destructive behavior by taking some first step on her own behalf. Obtaining help with her addiction, leaving the street for a shelter, or attempting to break off from an abusive and exploitive relationship with the oppressing partner may be the first step in breaking out of her trap. Each step that she takes in her own self-interest, however small, can contribute to a more positive feeling about herself and strengthen her for the next step. Thus, managing one's feelings helps one to manage one's problems, and managing one's problems helps to manage feelings.

The Integration of the Personal and Professional Self

When social work adopted the medical model, one of the concepts borrowed was the importance of maintaining one's professional role. Most helping professions stressed the professional role and the need to suppress personal feelings and reactions. For example, to work with stressful patients, one might have to keep one's impulses in check so as to avoid appearing judgmental. A professional worker was described as one who would maintain control of emotions and thus would not become angry or too emotionally involved, would not cry in the presence of a client, and so forth. The mandate to the worker appeared to be, Take your professional self to work and leave your personal self at home. This image of professionalism was widely held with many of the author's social work students starting their careers, wondering if they would have problems becoming a social worker because they "felt too much."

The interactional practice model suggests that we have been faced with a false dichotomy when we were forced to choose between our personal self and our professional self. In fact, the author will argue that we are at our best in our work when we are able to synthesize the two—that is, when we integrate our personal self with our professional role.

This conflict in view of the professional self surfaced in a workshop the author led on direct practice. One hospital social worker described an incident in which a mother appeared at her door after being referred by the attending physician. The mother had just been told that her seven-year-old daughter had a terminal illness. After explaining this to the social worker, the mother broke down and cried.

When the author asked the worker how she responded, she described how overwhelmed she felt by the mother's grief. All that the worker could do was to sit and hold the mother's hand, and to cry with her. The author maintained that although there would be much work to be done in this case (e.g., helping the mother deal with the dying daughter and her family over the next few months), at this point, what the mother needed most was not advice but someone to be with her. In fact, as the worker partially experienced the mother's pain and shared it with her through her own tears, she was giving that client an important gift of her own feelings. The worker was being professional in the best sense of that word. Other workers, who might not cry as easily with a client, might make the same gift in other noverbal ways—facial expressions, a respectful silence, a hand on the shoulder, each worker responding in a way consistent with his or her own personality. The crucial factor would be the worker's willingness to be honest and to share his or her own feelings.

In this case, the worker continued her story by stating that her supervisor, who had walked past the open door, called her out and berated her for unprofessional behavior. The supervisor said, "How could you let yourself break down that way? You can't help your clients if you become overwhelmed yourself." When the author asked the worker what she took from the experience, she replied, "I learned to keep my door closed."

Although many who hear this story may be upset with the supervisor, the author was not. He realized that she may have been trained, as the author was, in a time when any personal expression of emotion was considered to be unprofessional. He would have encouraged the worker to talk to her supervisor because it was crucial for her to obtain support from her supervisor and colleagues if she were to continue to provide this kind of help to clients. The author's most recent research (Shulman, 1991) has emphasized the importance of formal and informal sources of social support for social workers. This worker was making a gift to the client of her willingness to be with her at a terrible moment in the client's life. The worker's capacity to continue to be there for the client will be somewhat dependent on her having someone—supervisor, colleagues, or both—there for her.

This artificial split between the personal and professional selves was created because of the profession's understandable concern over the *inappropriate* use of self by helping professionals. For example, social work educators were concerned about countertransference or unfinished business. They were also troubled by workers who use the argument of spontaneity to justify acting out with clients, getting inappropriately angry or judgmental, or sharing personal problems. ("If you think you have troubles with your wife let me tell you about my marriage.") Unethical behavior with clients, such as exploiting the powerful forces of the helping bond to sexually exploit a vulnerable client, is another example. Fear of expression of feelings and points of view that are racist, sexist, homophobic, and so forth, is another area of concern. Each of these examples illustrates the lack of integration of personal and professional selves. The concerns about the inappropriate use of the personal self are well-founded. Unfortunately, the adopted solution to isolate our personal from our professional self leads to more problems than it resolves.

The argument advanced throughout this guide will be that each of us brings to our professional practice our own personal style, artistry, background, feelings, values, beliefs, and so on. Rather than denying or suppressing these, we need to learn more about ourselves in the context of our practice, and learn to use our self in pursuit of our professional functions. We will make many mistakes along the way, saying things we will later regret, having to apologize to clients, learning from these mistakes, correcting them, and then making more sophisticated mistakes. In other words, we will be real people carrying out difficult jobs as best we can, rather than paragons of virtue who present an image of perfection.

As we demonstrate to our clients our humanness—vulnerability, willingness to risk, spontaneity, honesty—and our lack of defensiveness (or defensiveness for which we later apologize), we will be modeling the very behaviors we hope to see in our clients. Thus, when workers or students ask, Should I be professional or should I be myself? the answer is that *the dichotomy implied in the question does not exist*. They must be themselves if they are going to be professional. Fortunately, they have the whole of their professional lives to learn how to effect the synthesis.

As this model is explored, it will be presented that a crucial skill for the worker, if she or he is to help clients to manage their feelings, will be the worker's ability to manage his or her own emotions. For example, in practice with survivors of sexual abuse, the worker, feeling clients' pain, may prematurely attempt to reassure them that they are not damaged. Or, the worker may take on survivors' anger against the oppressor, an act that may preempt clients' essential work in facing their own anger. Both understandable emotional reactions by the worker may block clients' ability to manage their own feelings. The worker would need to share his or her sense of clients' pain without trying to relieve it. For example:

> As I listen to you, I'm feeling how much pain you are in, how damaged you must feel. A big part of me wants to say "Don't feel that way! You are a person of value." But I know that no matter what I say the pain is there, and I can't make it go away.

The anger against exploitive men, for example, a sexually abusive father, can also be shared, but in a manner that helps the client to face her own anger rather than doing the work for her.

> It makes me angry when I think of what was done to you by people you expected to take care of you and to protect you. But from what you are saying to me, it seems that your feelings are mixed right now. It sounds like a big part of you wishes your family could be different—that they could change and that you could still be like a real family.

The sharing of the worker's feelings, in an integration of personal and professional self, will be a crucial element in this model.

Skills for Helping Clients to Manage Their Feelings and Problems

The eight skills examined in the author's recent studies (Shulman, 1991, 1992) were drawn from those that proved to be most important in previous research (Shulman, 1978, 1979).[1] The list below summarizes the two sets of skills:

SKILLS FOR HELPING CLIENTS TO MANAGE THEIR FEELINGS
- Reaching Inside of Silences
- Putting the Client's Feelings Into Words
- Displaying Understanding of Client's Feelings
- Sharing Worker's Feelings

SKILLS FOR HELPING CLIENTS TO MANAGE THEIR PROBLEMS
- Clarifying Worker's Purpose and Role
- Reaching for Client Feedback
- Partializing Client Concerns
- Supporting Clients in Taboo Areas

All of these skills are important in all phases of practice. However, each skill may be varied and may also have another meaning, or a varying impact, at different stages in the relationship. Because the helping process is so complex, it helps to analyze it in the context of the phases of work. The four phases of work described in this guide are:

1. Preliminary (or Preparatory) Phase
2. Beginning (or Contracting) Phase
3. Middle (or Work) Phase
4. Ending and Transition Phase

Each phase of work—preliminary, beginning, middle, and ending and transition—has unique dynamics and requires specific skills. The *preliminary phase* is the time period prior to the first encounter with the client. The *beginning phase* refers to the initial sessions in which the worker develops a working contract with the client. The *middle phase* focuses on the work to be done. Finally, in the *ending and transition phase*, the worker prepares the client to bring the relationship to an end and to make transitions to new experiences. The author will use the phases of work to organize the presentation of the core skills, starting with the preliminary phase.

Skills for Professional Performance

In an article on classroom teaching of social work practice, Schwartz (1964, p. 5) identified four categories of professional performance: (1) direct practice, (2) professional impact, (3) job management, and (4) continued learning.

---

[1] There were 22 communication, relationship, and problem-solving skills examined in the first analysis, all of which were seen as useful tools for practice.

Direct practice refers to the work of helping professionals in either a clinical or community setting, with clients in any system—individual, couple, family, and group. This practice calls for skills in communicating, relationship building, problem solving, and assessing and working with these individuals, families, or groups. *Professional-impact* skills are required at two levels: The first level refers to the skills needed to work effectively with other professionals on behalf of specific clients. For example, conversations with physicians, teachers, or social workers in other agencies to obtain a service for a client. The second, those required to implement a course of action designed to make one's professional contribution to the processes of social change—in the agency, in the neighborhood, and in the profession itself. *Job management* skills include those required to organize a practice, such as the recording of experience, the collection of data, the scheduling of appointments, the completion of required forms, and so forth. Finally, *continued learning* includes the skills required to incorporate resources such as supervision, the literature, and exchange with colleagues and specialists in a personal approach to professional problem solving and ongoing professional development.

This structure of professional performance is useful in conceptualizing the broad learning areas involved in professional education supervision. This guide focuses on the teaching of skills for professional practice and continued learning.

The role of mediator is an essential one in the interactional concept of supervision (Shulman, 1993).[2] In teaching the skills required in these categories of professional performance, the supervisor's role is that of a mediator between the learner (the subject of the learning process) and the ideas to be learned (the objects). Dewey (1916) was one of the first to recognize the possibilities of such a functional role, noting that "the teacher should be occupied not with the subject matter itself but with its interaction with the pupils' present needs and capacities" (p. 74).

In this guide, the concept of mediation function, derived from Schwartz's work, has been applied to the practice of supervision. The supervisor's role is seen as that of mediator between the student and the systems with which they must deal—the agency, colleagues, the client, or the community—and the subject areas to be taught. Likewise, the objective of social work education is to prepare the student to eventually help clients negotiate the various systems of demand they encounter.

---

[2] This concept is also suggested as a function of the helping person in the author's text on practice skills, *The Skills of Helping Individuals, Families and Groups* (3rd ed.), Itasca, IL: F. E. Peacock, 1992.

TEACHING CORE PRACTICE SKILLS

The mediation character of the teaching function can be utilized by supervisors to help students develop core communication, relationship, and problem-solving skills. Here, the focus is on these skills as they are applied by the student in direct practice, with implications for the educational function of supervision. Each skill is illustrated by a verbatim account describing how a student or worker has employed it with a client, followed by a section on supervision approaches that suggests how supervisors can teach the skill. These suggested approaches are also illustrated with verbatim reports, and the ways in which supervisors can model use of the skill for workers are pointed out.

The skills discussed from these viewpoints include those of tuning in, contracting, and dealing with the authority theme, as well as the skill factors (groupings) of empathy, elaboration, making a demand for work, sharing one's feelings, and sharing data. In addition, the skills required for dealing with the ending and transition phase are presented. These are the key skills required by beginning workers in most helping relationships and also the most adaptable to teaching through modeling by supervisors.[3]

Tuning In and Responding Directly to Indirect Cues

Many of the important communications shared by clients, particularly in "taboo" areas such as authority and sex, are expressed indirectly. Clients will often hint at a concern that they are afraid to express openly. The tuning-in skill helps students put themselves in the place of the client as a way of developing preliminary empathy.

A key question clients often have when first meeting a worker is, What kind of worker will this person be? They may be concerned that workers will judge them harshly and not understand their feelings. Parents, for example, may ask workers they have just met whether they are married and have children, as an indirect way of finding out if the worker can understand their concerns. Students who respond by providing a detailed description of their training can turn these clients off in the first interview. If they are tuned into the implicit meaning of this question, they can, however, use the skill of responding directly to an indirect cue. A student could say, for example, "No, I'm not married. Why do you ask? Are you worried that I might not understand what it's like for you to raise kids?" Such an invitation encourages clients to be more direct about their concerns, and it gives students an

---

[3] A more complete discussion and illustrations of these skills, and others, can be found in the author's text on practice skills, *The Skills of Helping Individuals, Families and Groups* (3rd ed.). See also "Core Skills for Field Instructors" in Appendix C, *Videotape Programs on Practice and Field Instruction*.

opportunity to demonstrate an understanding of the difficulty they are experiencing in the encounter. As a result, this can help develop a more positive relationship between them.

Students can tune in to a range of possible feelings and concerns on the client's part and prepare to reach for them. Tuning in is tentative, however. Students must be prepared to abandon preconceived ideas about what clients might feel and to respond instead to the reality of the interview. The preparation of tuning in gives students a better chance of responding to indirect communications instead of reacting defensively.

Supervision approaches. Supervisors can teach the skill of tuning in by providing an exercise to prepare workers for a first interview. Students should be encouraged to strive to connect to the feelings of clients by remembering a similar instance in their own experience when they sought help from some professional. The exercise becomes a form of role play, in which the students try to tune in to clients' underlying feelings. As they do this, they should also tune in to their own feelings, for example, nervousness at being new to the job or concern about having enough professional or life experience to be able to help a client.

Supervisors can help by understanding and directly reaching for students' feelings about being in training. If supervisors can remember what it was like at the start of their own practice, they are more likely to be supportive of students. If supervisors are themselves tuned in and respond directly to the feelings of new students, they will thus demonstrate the importance of these two skills for workers. Supervisors' modeling of these skills is the most effective way of teaching them.

In the following example, a supervisor tries to respond to a student's feelings of panic when called by a new client who is herself in a panic. The client, Mrs. Cohen, was extremely upset and had called the student to demand that she find an immediate placement for John, a six-year-old child. Mrs. Cohen claimed she was no longer able to handle the child and did not know what to do if the agency could not get John off her hands. The student, Susan, was so upset herself that she panicked and told the client she would call her back after she phoned her supervisor.

The supervisor's account of how *she* tried to tune in to the student's feelings during the telephone conversation and help her develop a strategy for handling the client are included in the following notes:

> Susan said she felt overwhelmed by Mrs. Cohen's (the client) demands and didn't know how she should respond. I went on to explain that it was not Susan's role to provide solutions, instead she should work to explore Mrs. Cohen's feelings, the options she could envisage, their possible consequences, and so on.
>
> I stopped talking, and there was silence on the other end. I told her that I was quiet to allow her to raise concerns I might not yet had addressed. She said she was thinking how she would say this to Mrs. Cohen. She told me she had copied down everything I was saying. I acknowledged her problem in that she had my words but that it is hard to feel good about using someone else's words.
>
> STUDENT: I'd like to be able to tell her something. Mrs. Cohen feels that the psych assessment unit and our work with her hasn't done any good, because she's still got the problem. I really feel terrible.
>
> SUPERVISOR: Your Mrs. Cohen seems to have misunderstood what you, the assessment team, or any other helping person is able to do, and you're feeling bad in recognizing how limited we, as helping persons, are. We can only help Mrs. Cohen work out ways of coping with her problems, we can't come up with her answers.
>
> STUDENT: I'll try to think about all these things and get all my "social working" notions put together before I call her this evening.

SUPERVISOR: That's good, but don't let *your* concerns get in the way of being able to hear *her* concerns.

STUDENT: But what if she still wants to put John in a foster home like she did this morning?

SUPERVISOR: Mrs. Cohen was in a panic and was proposing a panic solution, and it sounds like you're getting caught in her panic.

STUDENT: That's exactly where I am!

SUPERVISOR: I figured that. Let's look at what panic does. It crowds your mind so you can't think. There's one idea that gets stuck in your head, and you can't think your way past it.

STUDENT: Yes, that's how I feel.

SUPERVISOR: So now we need to figure out a way to help Mrs. Cohen past her panic over the thought of foster placement.

I proceeded to talk about what Susan could do to lower Mrs. Cohen's anxiety level and her own, until they were both calm enough to consider a whole range of options and critically explore their respective advantages and disadvantages. She said, "That sounds good."

I went on to suggest to Susan that going through this exercise with Mrs. Cohen and exploring this process with her is ever so much more helpful to Mrs. Cohen than trying to solve her problem for her. Learning how to cope with and overcome panic so that she can deal with the issues in a reasonable way will, in the long run, be much more beneficial to Mrs. Cohen than her frantic pursuit of answers.

My impression was that Susan was beginning at this point to overcome her own panic and was starting to think constructively as to how she would deal with this evening's interview or phone contact. Susan was told to contact me at home in the evening.

Contracting

In the beginning phase of work, the client is probably wondering, What's this all about? An important part of the student's preparation includes planning to clarify the potential working contract with the client during the first interview. Three critical skills for the student in contracting are (1) clarifying purpose or role, (2) reaching for feedback, and (3) dealing with the authority theme. The first two of these skills are discussed in this section, and the authority of the worker is the topic of the following one.

A general problem in the helping professions is that of *clarifying purpose and role*, or defining precisely what the worker is to do. In the case of family workers, which will be used to illustrate the contracting skills, it is not unusual for students to be unclear about what they are supposed to offer a family. A first interview will be uncomfortable under the best of circumstances for both the student and the members of the family, but this discomfort will be increased if there is doubt about the student's role. To set the client quickly at ease, it is helpful for the student to prepare a brief opening statement describing the reason for the referral and the services that can be offered.

The following material drawn from an actual interview illustrates the skills of clarifying purpose and role in action. It is an example of a first contact with Mrs. Henry, a 28-year-old mother of three children. After being introduced by Mrs. Henry's social worker, the family worker attempted to explain her purpose in these words:

I thought it would help if I took a moment to explain why I have been asked to work with your family. John (the social worker) has told me things are rough right now for you, with a lot of concerns on your mind. I understand it has been upsetting for you

> since your husband left, and with your oldest boy having trouble at school, it is easy to understand how these things can pile up. John felt that if I could spend some time with your family, there might be some ways I could take some of the load off of you. For example, I would be glad to talk with you if the going gets rough some days with the kids. I could listen and maybe help you figure out what to do about some of the problems the kids are making for you. If you thought it would be helpful, I would be glad to go down to the school and see what is going on with your boy, Frank. Maybe if I talked to the counselor, and the teacher, and then Frank, I could help get him back in. Does any of this sound like it might be helpful from your point of view?

By beginning this way, the worker has been direct about her purpose and has also provided some "handles" for work—suggestions of ways she might help. These handles partialize the problems and provide some concrete indications of what the worker means by her offer to help. This directness helps clients to quickly sort out how workers might help, and it decreases clients' concern that workers are there to do something to them. Workers are often embarrassed at being direct with clients; they fear coming on too strong and turning the client off, or they begin with a notion of their role as that of "changing" the client. They have a hidden agenda that explains their reluctance to be direct. Because clients do not lend themselves to being "changed," the sooner the worker gives up this hidden agenda, the quicker a more honest working relationship can develop.

Reaching for feedback is important because the client has to accept the offer of service. In this example, Mrs. Henry may pick up on only one part of the contract—the part she feels urgency about or is willing to risk, often a near problem, one close to the more difficult concerns. Alternatively, she may be ready to trust the worker and to deal with more serious problems instead of near problems. It is important to recognize that the worker can only help in those areas in which the client feels some sense of investment and a freedom to risk. Mrs. Henry began to take the family worker up on the offer, as the worker reported:

> Mrs. H. said that things had been rough and that the school problem just was the last straw. Frank had been suspended for not doing homework and fighting in the classroom. I told her that I thought that must have come as quite a blow. She said she just didn't know what to do. She was at her wit's end. She found herself getting angry at her son when he hung around the house.

With the feedback from the client, the work has begun. Because the worker is willing to listen and to respond with some empathy, an important start is being made on the working relationship, a necessity for creating the conditions in which the client will use the worker's help.

Although the specifics of the purpose and the role may differ according to the situations in which help is provided, contracting skills are crucial to all helping situations. In the following example of a first session between a worker and a foster adolescent, it would not be surprising if the client refused an offer put in these terms by the worker:

> Since I'm going to be your new worker, I wanted to meet you to find out how things were going with you, and to see if there was anything I might be able to help with. I know that you have been moving around a lot this past year and that starting in a new foster home and at a new school with new friends can be difficult. How about it, how has it been?

In this case, a working relationship has not been formed yet, and the client may not trust the worker. In addition, the client may not feel that there are any difficulties to discuss. Nevertheless, the worker has made the offer, and the client heard it. Later, if problems emerge, or if the trust develops, the client may be more ready to use the worker's help.

Clarifying purpose and role is also essential in a brief, limited-focus interview. An example is the following comments made by a social work student to a hospital patient about to be discharged:

> Your doctor has told me that you are about to be discharged. He was concerned that it might be difficult for you when you return home, because you have been through a tough time here at the hospital. I wanted to see if I might be helpful in any way— perhaps by sending a homemaker or someone to help out with the kids until you get settled back in. Is there anything you are concerned about?

As the client describes the situation, it is often possible to identify other areas in which services may be helpful. A student might pick up the idea, for example, that a single parent is having difficulty dealing with her children and suggest a referral to a family agency.

This discussion is not meant to suggest that contracting is a mechanical process for the student. Each one approaches first sessions differently, and each must respond to the unique nature of her or his client's responses. A student might find that the client is eager to talk and that the student needs to listen first, before stating what he or she has to offer. The important point is that at some time in the first interview, the discussion should focus on the connections between the client's felt needs and the service that the agency or other setting can provide.

Supervision approaches. One of the best ways for the supervisor to help a new student get ready to make a first contact with a client is to suggest a role play in which the student tries out an opening statement of purpose and role. The supervisor can then respond in a number of ways, preparing the student for possible reactions. The student's opening statement often reveals a lack of clarity, and the supervisor can help the student rethink her or his purpose and role. The use of jargon instead of precise terms and meaningful expressions can be pointed out, and the student can be helped to think of alternatives. The role play will often reveal many of the student's fears about the encounter, giving the supervisor an opportunity to discuss them.

This exercise can provide the student with the confidence to be more relaxed in the first session and thus less defensive. It may reveal the student's feelings in the situation, feelings that can have an influence on willingness to offer help to a client. The student is often reluctant to contract with the client in this way, for example, if he or she foresees the involuntary removal of a child as a distinct possibility. When the supervisor inquires about the student's attitude toward the client, it turns out that the student is afraid of feeling like a "rat" if he or she encourages a client to open up and then has to suggest the removal of the child.

Another way of helping students is to follow up after an interview in order to discuss the details of the encounter. The student could write up notes describing the discussion, or, if time does not permit, attempt to recall the dialogue from memory. The supervisor must ask about some of the details for the interaction to be helpful. If the student comments on the client's defensiveness, for example, the supervisor should request an account of what both client and student said. Often, even a few moments of discussion will help a student and supervisor understand the interaction in a new way. As the student begins to see the client's actions as responses to his or her intervention, the focus can shift from discussion of the case to discussion of the student's skills.

There is an interesting parallel between this form of supervision and the work done with clients. For example, when a parent discusses a problem with a teenaged child, the student, like the supervisor, should ask for the details of the encounter—what the client actually said and how the child responded. The student can be most helpful by examining the specifics of the parent-child interaction, and the same is true for the supervisor. This skill, which is called moving from the general to the specific, is one of the most important, and yet often overlooked skills for increasing the effectiveness of supervision. (It is discussed in more detail later under the elaboration skills section.) Perhaps as a result of the medical paradigm that has guided our professional theory development, supervisors often become preoccupied with the assessment and diagnosis stage of work focusing on the case rather than on the process of interaction. Intervention suggestions may remain at a general level with limited attention to the actual conversation. One advantage of this interactional paradigm is that it forces both the supervisor and the student to focus on the particulars of the practice.

A process recording can be a very useful teaching device for getting at the process of practice. In one approach, the student would write a brief description of the conversation at the start of the session, including some verbatim dialogue. A summary would describe what followed, with expanded detailed descriptions of crucial aspects of the middle of the session. The ending would also be written verbatim, for a total process recording of two pages.

Unfortunately, in the helping professions, the idea of paying attention to the details of the work through the use of some form of process or audiovisual recording has been losing favor among supervisors. A number of years ago, the writing of process records was considered students' work, a task that was quickly dropped after graduation. New workers who had requested help from supervisors with such recordings were often told to realize they were in the real world where such devices were luxuries, or even worse, they were accused of being overly dependent. More recently, the trend has been to abandon the use of recording even in the professional school setting. In the author's field instructors' workshops, many graduates comment that they did not write a single process recording in their two years of training.

This state of affairs is both ironic and alarming. It is ironic because recording and attention to detail were very much a part of early professional practices at a time when the ability to conceptualize practice skills was still at an infant stage. While practice was being examined in detail, often it was without the analytic tools required for the job. Now that many middle-range models of practice from a number of theoretical frameworks are available, the tendency seems to be to move away from examining practice. This trend is alarming—because in working with clients or supervising students, it is impossible to develop practice skills without some ongoing means of examining the details of one's practice efforts.

One event that ran contrary to the tide was the publication of a book on guidelines for recording by Suanna J. Wilson (1980). This book examined a number of types of recording in some detail and provided many illustrations that can be useful for supervisors who want to strengthen their students' recording efforts. It also provided a model that supervisors can adapt for recording their own supervision practice.

When the author discusses the recording issue with supervisors in his workshops, their first response is usually to argue that neither the student nor the supervisor has the time to record all of his or her work in such detail. The author agrees with the point, but suggests, however, that selecting cases or supervision interviews for periodic recording is practicable. Although most supervisors agree, they then point out how time-consuming that writing and reading full process recordings can be. This is also true, so the author offers a manageable alternative— a shortened version of the process recording, described by William Schwartz as the *accordion style*, in which the beginning, middle, and the ending of a session are written in detailed process, with summary descriptions providing the links. (The term *accordion* describes the expansion and contraction of the detailed portions of the record.) The total writing might be less than two pages.

Student resistance is the next problem with recording that supervisors often raise. This initiates a discussion of the meaning of such resistance and how to handle it by encouraging student elaboration of past experience (sometimes negative) and current plans as to how the recording will be used. Many supervisors admit they have had bad experiences themselves with recording—submitting records the supervisor never read, or having detailed supervisory comments that were critical, or punitive, added to the margins of their recordings. One supervisor said she had learned quickly not to write down what she had really said in an encounter, but what she thought the supervisor would have wanted her to say. Certainly, such experiences cause ambivalent feelings about the procedure when the supervisor is faced with student resistance to this method.

One of the most serious concerns about introducing recording into the supervision process was put this way by one supervisor: "If I ask my students to write records, I'm going to have to come through and offer them help." This fear of not being up to the task is common with supervisors who feel they must provide answers to their students rather than suggesting a way of working. I try to reassure them that it is all right to be teaching and learning at the same time and that students will still respect them when they honestly share their own struggles with recording events. One supervisor described how he was process recording his own conferences with students so he could become comfortable with the tool in his own work, before he set expectations for recording for his students. He has shared this with his students, even showing them his beginning efforts. They were impressed with his willingness to risk himself.

Another important way the supervisor teaches the contracting skills is by demonstrating them in the supervision context. In early interviews with a new worker, the supervisor should first clarify the purpose of supervision and the role of the supervisor and then attempt to reach for worker feedback. The supervisor can also prepare an opening statement to begin the contracting with the student. The contract will inevitably be broad, because the supervisor has many responsibilities. But the part of the contract concerning the development of practice skills might be stated like this:

> Part of what I will be doing with you is helping you look at the way you work with clients. When you are getting ready to go out on first interviews, I can help you prepare by thinking through what you might say. After an interview, particularly one you feel you had trouble with, I will be glad to listen to what went on and to try to help you figure out what you did right and what you might have done differently. In addition, there will be some days when the work gets rough and you're feeling low. If you want someone to talk to, I'll try to be available to listen.

There are a number of reasons why supervisors often ignore the specifics of students' interactions with their clients. Some may not have experienced this kind of work themselves, or they may have had bad experiences with punitive discussions regarding their practice. They were not allowed to make mistakes. Others refrain from this work because they sense resistance from the student. Still others are afraid to make this offer because they feel they would not be able to respond adequately if the student were to ask for help. But it is not really necessary for supervisors to have all of the answers. What supervisors can provide are ways of working on the questions, some insight from their own experiences, and some support for the student in the struggle. In parallel, this is *exactly* what the students will be offering the client.

The problem of limited time is often appropriately cited by supervisors who have many demands placed upon them. In reality, however, they may have to spend a great deal of time dealing with the problems created by the lack of student skill. For example, a breakdown in the placement of a teenager may have been indirectly hinted at by the client but not picked up by the student who had contracted poorly with the client. This problem may then demand many hours of time and much energy, all of which might have been avoided. Another situation that might never have arisen had the student developed more skillfully the initial working relationship with the frightened mother is the apprehension of an abused child. This also takes its toll on both time and emotions.

Dealing With the Authority of the Worker

Whenever a client first comes into contact with a helping person, the tendency of the client is to perceive that person as an authority figure. This is true even in situations in which the client is a voluntary one or does not fear the worker's legal authority. The client transfers to the new encounter feelings and perceptions derived from past experiences with people in authority—parents, teachers, and other workers. The worker must be sensitive to how the theme of authority affects the client and be prepared to discuss it directly if it blocks the working relationship. Because authority is a taboo subject, the student may have to help the client feel comfortable enough to discuss it. The necessity of discussing this relationship periodically should be anticipated. In this sense, the authority theme may represent an obstacle to work. In addition to the possibility of transference by clients, students should guard against the countertransference of their own feelings and perceptions from past experiences with clients. It is not uncommon for young students to identify with children in a family conflict situation, for example, because they perceive the parents in a stereotyped fashion and thus loose their sense of function. This may lead them to take sides, which cuts them off as helpers to the parents.

In situations in which the agency does carry clear authority or statutory responsibility over the life of the client, as in child abuse cases, it is essential to deal with the authority theme early in the relationship. Defensive or hostile clients often have a stereotyped idea of workers, based on past experiences or on what they have heard from other clients. A client's underlying image of a worker as, for example, a "baby snatcher" may manifest itself in hostile behavior.

A student meeting this kind of response should deal with it directly, as a start to contracting. The following report illustrates this:

> I told her I had come because we had calls from her neighbors who were concerned that she might be having difficulties with her kids. I told her I wanted to see if this

were true and if there were any way I could help. The client responded angrily and defensively, saying her neighbors were lying and out to get her. She told me that what went on with her kids was none of my business and that she would rather not talk to me about it.

I told her it was obvious that she was upset because I was there. I went on to say that it wasn't easy for me, either. I asked her if she was worried that we might be thinking of taking her kids from her. She told me in a very angry voice that she wouldn't let me if I tried. I told her that we often get calls from neighbors and that just getting a call did not mean we would remove children from families. I told her that we were more interested in helping kids stay in families and that it was only under serious circumstances—for example, when children were being beaten or neglected or their parents were having problems with the kids that we could not help with—that we would consider apprehending children. That was not what we wanted. We would much rather help parents out with their problems so that the kids could stay at home.

I asked her why she was so upset at my being there. Had she had experiences with social workers before? She said she had not, but a neighbor of hers had. She went on to describe an incident in which the worker had removed a child. I first told her I could understand why she had been so upset and worried when I arrived. I asked her if we could start all over and then shared that we had lots of parents who came to us because the going was rough with the kids. When you're alone with three kids, and they're after you all day, and you can't get out because you have no help, it's easy to understand how you could get angry and lose your temper. There was a long silence. She was staring at my face, probably trying to decide whether to believe me or not. She finally said it was rough sometimes. I asked if she would like to tell me a bit about the rough times.

There are many clients who will not accept the student's offer of help, particularly in a stressful situation such as fearing the apprehension of a child. It may take a long time for some clients to believe a student, however, it is important for the student to make the offer. Unless direct statements of purpose and role are made in the beginning stage of work, the sessions will be constantly hindered by lack of clarity of contract.

Supervision approaches. The parallels between the supervisor-student and the student-client relationships are obvious when dealing with the authority theme. The authority of the supervisor can have a powerful impact on the working relationship. By monitoring this issue and encouraging students to be open with them, supervisors can effectively demonstrate the skills required for addressing authority directly. Early in the working relationship, the field instructor should encourage discussion about the student's comfort about confronting the supervisor, being honest, and so on. It is more than likely, however, that it will take some time before the student actually trusts the invitation. An alert field instructor will pick up on any indirect cues of the student's cautiousness and use that as an opportunity for work on the issue of the authority theme in their relationship.

In the following example, the supervisor provided feedback on a client interview in which the student had suggested that a client in a child welfare setting attend a parent-effectiveness training program. The client had quickly agreed. In discussing the interview, the supervisor had questioned whether the client had willingly agreed to such or was simply providing the response she thought the student wanted to hear. The supervisor had suggested that the student explore the client's teal feelings during the next session, encouraging the client to openly express any reservation she had about attending the course. The student agreed; but in a role play, when the field instructor (playing the client) quickly responded positively, the student again accepted the client's agreement.

SUPERVISOR: In my role play as client, you were quick to accept my agreement to attend the session. How come?

STUDENT: I think the client really does want to go to the session. If I ask the client for her reservations, I might upset her, and then she will change her mind.

SUPERVISOR: So you are actually afraid that if you were to explore her ambivalence about the program, it might become a self-fulfilling prophecy.

STUDENT: Right!

SUPERVISOR: Why didn't you say that earlier when I first suggested that she may not really have agreed with you? (Silence.)

STUDENT: Well, you are the supervisor.

SUPERVISOR: (Laughing.) So here I am trying to get you to explore your client's reluctance to be honest with you, while, at the same time, you're not sure you can level with me. What makes it so difficult for you to disagree with me?

STUDENT: Well, let's face it, you're going to grade me. Maybe you are right. I mean, I'm only a student, and I'm not so sure about these things.

SUPERVISOR: Good! Now we are getting somewhere. Let me reassure you that one of the things I'm going to be very positive about, in terms of your evaluation, is your ability to be honest with me, to take risks, and to take me on when you disagree. I would be more worried if I felt you were always agreeing just to please me. And the point is, how are we going to be able to effectively explore these issues if you hold back on your real views and feelings. As far as your uncertainty, it's important that you develop your own views and your own understanding about how to work with clients. I'll share my opinions, but with very few exceptions, you're not required to agree. Try me out with some safer disagreements, and see how I do. I'll try to make sure I continue to encourage you to take me on. How does that sound?

STUDENT: It sounds okay, but it may take a while for me to learn how to do this. It's quite diferent from how I have related to supervisors before.

After such a discussion, it is often helpful to point out to students that the parallel process occurs in the client-student, versus student-supervisor, relationship and to remind the student that the client probably feels the same toward the student as the student now feels toward the supervisor.

SUPERVISOR: We will make it an agenda item for monitoring as we go along. Now, I'm wondering if this conversation we just had has some relevance for your work with Ms. Smith.

STUDENT: You mean she may be holding back from me in the same way I did with you? (Silence.) So I have to talk to her about her being more direct with me—is that what you're saying?

Empathy Skills

A central assumption about the use of empathy is that the way people feel is related to how they act and that the way people act will affect how they feel. For example, parents who feel lonely and unhappy and who judge themselves harshly will often express these feelings in the way they act toward their children. For example, a parent's tension can lead the child to act out his or her feelings through negative behavior that, in turn, causes the parent to be less tolerant. A vicious cycle develops. To take another example, a mother on welfare, whose children have grown up, feels she would like to go back to work and consults an employment counselor about available opportunities. If she feels inadequate about reentering the work force after so many years at home, however, she may act this out by missing job interviews. Such a client is ambivalent: on the one hand, she wants independence and self-respect, and on the other, she is afraid to take the risk. Likewise, an adolescent who has been rejected by his family and has moved through a number of foster homes no longer believes he can have a stable, close relationship with adults. Because he has been hurt so often, he refuses to risk. He then begins new contacts in a residential treatment home with acting-out behavior, which brings about the rejection he fears. A hospital patient who is anxious about an impending medical procedure also may express the feeling through demanding or hostile behavior. In each of these cases, clients' feelings affect their actions, and their actions further affect their feelings.

Because of this connection between feeling and doing, there is a need for workers to be sensitive to the affective portion of a client's message. Unfortunately, in our society the open expression of feelings is somewhat of a taboo, and the norms under which most people operate forbid direct expression of some of their most difficult feelings. Workers need to develop skills that will help clients become more aware of their real feelings and be willing to share them. The workers' efforts to understand a client's feelings, and to experience them, will strengthen the worker-client relationship. The three empathy skills discussed in this section are (1) reaching for feelings, (2) acknowledging feelings, and (3) articulating the client's feelings or putting them into words.

Reaching for feelings involves listening to a client's description of a problem and asking about the associated feelings. For example, a mother describes a conflict situation with a daughter who had come home at 2 A.M. without having let the mother know where she was. The worker might inquire, "What did you feel when your daughter arrived?" The intent is to encourage the client to express her affect, or feelings. It is important that the empathic efforts be genuine; the worker must be interested in understanding the feelings and not just ask about them in a ritualistic manner. For these skills to be effective, workers must attempt to actually feel, as best as they can, the emotions of their clients. To do this in a meaningful way, they need to become sensitized to their own affective responses during interviews.

The skill of *acknowledging feelings* calls for the worker to communicate acceptance and appreciation of the client's affect. This skill is demonstrated in an interview with a client who was fearful during the first interview and had responded defensively. Later, the worker reported:

> Mrs. Freed told me that she had been fearful of me in the first interview. She didn't feel she could trust me and tell me what was really on her mind. I told her I could easily understand that if I had been in her shoes, I would have been just as scared and upset.

A more sophisticated skill is *articulating the client's feelings* just before they are expressed by the client. In any relationship, particularly at the beginning, people are reluctant to share their real feelings. Workers who are tuned in to clients may be able to sense how they feel, even before clients say anything about it. When the worker articulates these feelings, two objectives are accomplished: In effect, clients are not only given permission to discuss their feelings but also the opportunity to perceive the worker as someone who understands. Even if clients do not acknowledge a feeling, having heard it expressed may be enough. Here is an example of this skill in action:

> Mr. Gregory asked me how long his youngsters would be in care. I told him for six months, or longer if he or his wife wanted to extend the agreement (a voluntary placement). He said it was a long time for the kids. I said, "And for you too." He went on to tell me that his son John was confused and sad. I said, "That must make it hard

for you to see him." He said it was, because he was not sure of what to say to him. I said, "You mean when he asks you when he is coming home?" He said, "Well, yeah."

This worker was tuned in to the feelings of natural parents, particularly the guilt involved when a child is placed in care. She understood that parents often feel so bad about the placement that they cannot face the question in the eyes of a child wanting to know when it will be possible to come home. Natural parents often avoid that question by not coming to visit their children who have been placed in care, by appearing to be cold and indifferent or by getting drunk before a visit. In this case, the worker is so tuned in to the client's feelings that she is able to state her affective hunches slightly ahead of him. She does this when she says: "That must make it hard for you to see him," and "You mean when he asks you when he is coming home?" The value of the skill is that the worker's empathic reaction encourages the client to risk the feelings.

In another example, a nurse spoke to a mother in a hospital emergency waiting room about her child, who had an eye injury, in these terms:

> MOTHER: How long will it take to find out what's wrong? I've been here for almost an hour.
> NURSE: I'm sorry it is taking so long. The doctor is examining your daughter right now. (Pause.) It's really hard waiting when you're frightened about your daughter's sight.
> MOTHER: (Starts to cry.) Oh God, if I had been watching her, it wouldn't have happened.
> NURSE: (After a few minutes, places her hand on the mother's shoulder.) It's okay to cry—it's very tough for parents to see their own child hurt and not know how badly. I can't give you any real information, but for what it's worth, she didn't look too bad to me when I took her in. I'll try to find out what's up, and I'll tell you as soon as I can.

In any expression of empathy, the feelings must be genuine. Many students have had training that has taught them to deal with feelings routinely. When the students themselves are not actually feeling anything, the clients quickly see these efforts as false. Students who simply echo a client's response, for example, are not helping. If the client says, for example, "I'm angry at the agency," and the student responds, "You're angry at the agency," the client has every right to say that he just told the student that and can't understand why it is being repeated.

A ritualistic question, such as, How do you feel about that? also seems lacking in meaning. Mechanical responses such as "I hear you saying that . . ." often turn off clients rather than helps them discuss their feelings. Students will develop their own personal styles of empathizing, but the key to the effectiveness of the skill is that, as best they can, they genuinely respond to the feelings of the client.

The author's research on practice has found that the worker's ability to acknowledge the client's feelings is one of the most important skills in encouraging positive working relationships and in being helpful to clients (Shulman, 1978, 1991, 1992). In addition, the ability to articulate the client's feelings before they are expressed appears to contribute to the establishment of a good working relationship. These tentative results support the notion that rather than not risk the feeling for fear of alienating a client or of overstepping his or her boundaries in articulating the client's views, workers would do better to err on the side of risking their intuitions. This would allow the client the opportunity to reject them.

Supervision approaches. It is with the empathy skills that supervisors can model the helping process most effectively. It is self-defeating for supervisors to tell students they are not empathic with their clients if, at the same time, they are not empathic with their students. In workshops, the author often employs an exercise for field instructors that illustrates this point. If in presenting an example a supervisor is upset with a student for not being more supportive in her or his interaction with a particular client, the author would ask the group: "Who is this supervisor with right now?" It is usually clear to all that the supervisor has identified, at the moment, with the client. He then asks: "Who is with the student?" After a moment of silence, someone, often the presenting supervisor, will say, "Nobody!" It is very important that the author acknowledges during the discussion how hard it can be for the supervisor to be with the client *and* the student at the same time. This is the author's way of modeling the parallel process as he tries to be with both the supervisor and the student.

In the beginning phase of supervisory work, the supervisor can begin to demonstrate the importance of empathic responses by tuning in to the student's feelings and starting to articulate them when they first meet. Before a student's first interview, the supervisor might ask, "Are you worried about seeing your first client?" and later say something to the effect that "It must be scary wondering if you have anything to offer that client." Students will appreciate a supervisor's genuine effort to understand the experience and to support them during the tough times. The supervisor's articulation of these feelings also can free students to express their doubts and concerns.

Discussion of interviews is another instance when the supervisor's use of the empathic skills is helpful. As a student reports a client's comments, the supervisor might say, for example, "Do you remember what you were feeling at that moment?" Another approach would be to ask students to put themselves back into that moment in the interview and try to recall how it felt for them. By reaching for feelings, the supervisor indicates an interest in the student's affect during interviews. It is also helpful to explain that how the student feels during an interview is important to the supervisor. Often, what a student says is not related to what the student feels. Therefore, feelings affect what students do and say, just as they influence clients' behaviors.

Such discussions can lead students to consider what makes it difficult for them to articulate their own feelings. Because students are affected by the norms and taboos of our society, they may feel uncomfortable and embarrassed about discussing feelings. Although the student may be empathic with the client, the expression of this empathy is blocked. This is a normal response. Acknowledging the reasonableness of students' feelings may free them to deal with their clients more effectively.

Another helpful device is to ask students how an incident might be handled if it should recur. Sometimes simply attempting to express empathy in a role play can assist a student to find the right words to deal with a situation in practice.

The supervisor can also support students by pointing out that the ability to express empathy develops slowly and is influenced by age and experience, but it does eventually emerge. A student's capacity to express empathy for clients will grow with practice. As the supervisor examines cases when the student was not empathic or seemed distant, it may become apparent that another feeling was interfering with the student's capacity for empathy. Students who judge clients harshly because of their actions (e.g., child abuse) must learn to consider the clients as people with needs and problems of their own. In effect, students learn from their mistakes, and the supervisor's support and understanding will help them risk their feelings and feel more comfortable about learning in this way. There will be times when the student will be too depleted to empathize, or will be too rushed or upset; the supervisor has to acknowledge this. All these can also be problems for supervisors who themselves need support from their administrators and peers if they are to be able to help their workers.

The following excerpt shows how a supervisor helped a beginning student to examine her feelings about working with a father who had been accused of sexual abuse of a child. New students naturally bring a host of reactions to clients to the relationship, and supervisors must show them that they can admit to these feelings and begin to understand them more deeply. Students must learn to do two things simultaneously: first, to hold a client accountable for his or her behavior; second, to see past the behavior of the client and to tune into the client's feelings and concerns. The supervisor's report noted:

> Theresa began by presenting me with a case, in detail, that involved sexual abuse. She said, "That guy was really icky." I ask her what she meant by *icky*. She said, "Well, when Mr. Brown was standing near Jean, he put his hand on her head and she cringed." I observed she really had some feelings about Mr. Brown. She said emphatically, "I sure do hate him, the son of a bitch." I looked at her—silence. She said, "Whew! That was pretty strong!" I said, "Yeah, you sound really angry." She said, "I have angry feelings about abuse. I've seen too much of it . . . ."
>
> I asked her to tune into Mr. Brown and what he might be feeling. She said, "Mad." I asked, "How come?" She said, "Because we social workers were in his house." I asked what else. She said, "Maybe he feels icky, too." We talked about why he would feel icky. She concluded, "I really forgot to tune in to him and see him in the system. Another time I'll be more aware."

It would be important for a supervisor to work with a student about how to deal with these natural feelings in a professional manner rather than to pretend that they do not exist. In working with sexual abusers, for example, it may be helpful to be honest early in the relationship about the impact on the worker of what the client has done. To be able to admit to feeling angry about a client's actions, while simultaneously expressing a genuine concern about reaching out to the abuser as a client in his or her own right, is at the core of the ability to work with clients who hit us hard. In such powerful and emotion-laden situations, close monitoring by the supervisor and student of the potential for countertransference is crucial.

Each new type of client will generate new reactions in the worker, and the supervisor can help even experienced students by reaching for these feelings. In another example, senior male workers who were preparing to work with men who batter their partners had to look deeply into their own feelings about women and violence before they could honestly tune in to these clients. When audiotapes of interviews intended to prepare clients for the first group meeting were examined in some detail in a group supervision session, I pointed out that the worker had been lacking in empathy for a client and had seemed harsh and judgmental in a subtle way. This was true, even though the workers had indicated they felt they could accept these men as clients. The conversation continued as follows:

> I asked Frank why he had seemed so angry at the client—if he could put his finger on what he was feeling at the time. He indicated that he really hadn't realized he was feeling angry. I acknowledged that this was sometimes the hardest part—dealing with real feelings that are just beneath the surface. I asked if anyone else had any ideas.

Terry responded that Frank was probably really feeling angry at this guy for having beaten his old lady up that way—and that he knew we felt that way as well, even though we were trying to be nonjudgmental. I said, "Good, that's a start." Frank continued: "It's easy to say we shouldn't judge these guys, and I feel funny feeling this way, but I do get furious at them." I asked if they had any idea why this type of client hit them so hard. I told them I knew they were experienced workers and learned to handle tough problems, such as parental abuse of children. I wanted to know what was different with these men.

After a long pause, Frank said, "I think they remind me of my own anger toward women." I asked what he meant, and he explained that there were often times when he had felt so angry at his wife that he could have hit her—and that the difference between him and these clients was that he could control his anger and they couldn't. I said, "So when you see your own feelings in these men, it's very tough to face them— because they hit you so hard, and because it's tough to admit you have them." Terry said I had hit the nail on the head. I replied that I thought we were now starting to make a real start on tuning into these men, because they were being so honest in tuning into their own feelings.

Supervisors are often concerned about responding emphatically to students. Even those who have developed strong practice skills in this area and have little hesitation about being empathic with clients may be afraid this could amount to "social working" their students. They recognize that students are not clients, and they feel it would be inappropriate to bring up areas of personal concern. Nevertheless, the feelings students have about their practice are directly related to how they deal with clients, and these feelings *must* be discussed. As long as the supervisor's sense of function is clear and the work stays within the boundaries of the supervision contract, students appreciate evidence that the supervisor understands their dilemmas, concerns, and feelings. And supervisors appreciate the same sort of understanding from their own supervisors as well.

Sessional Contracting

In direct practice as in supervision, sessional contracting involves an attempt at the beginning of each session to determine the central areas of concern. The assumption is that clients will only invest themselves in matters about which they feel a sense of urgency. This skill involves asking clients, at the beginning of each session, what they would like to discuss. Even if the worker has an agenda that must be dealt with during the session, this negotiating process reassures clients that their concerns will also be heard. In addition, because clients often employ indirect communications at the beginning of an interview, it is helpful to be tentative about the agenda so that the real concerns can be explored.

In the following example, a teenaged girl had approached the student for help in finding a foster home. The student began the session by negotiating the working contract but remained tentative about it. Rather than dealing with the first issue raised by the client, the worker used the sessional contracting skill to give the client an opportunity to get to a more difficult issue. The student noted:

Jean had opened the interview by telling me she had heard from friends that I would be able to help her get a foster home. She said that she wanted to leave home right away. I told her we often did help youngsters find foster homes, but first we had to be pretty clear that they were unable to live at home. I asked if she could tell me why she wanted to move out.

She presented a long description of a fight she'd been having with her mom, not being able to get enough clothing, hassles over the time she needs to get home in the evening, describing a generally difficult relationship. Although it sounded stressful, it didn't sound serious enough for Jean's sense of urgency. I told her that it sounded like she was having a hard time with her mom, but what she was describing didn't seem to be way out of line with the problems that happen in most families. I wondered if there was something else that was also troubling her. There was a silence, and then she said she doesn't like the men that hang around the house. I asked her if she could tell me a bit more about that. I noticed as she talked that she looked down and seemed embarrassed. She told me that there was a lot of activity with men at night in the room next to her. It was a small apartment, and she was very uncomfortable.

I told her I realized it wasn't easy to talk about these matters, but it would be important for me to know what was happening if I was to be able to help her. Acting on a hunch caused by her embarrassment, I asked if any of the men had been bothering her. She looked up quickly, seemed relieved, and said that her mom's latest boyfriend had been making passes at her.

Had the student simply responded to the first issue, she might have explored the concern simply as a problem between Jean and her mother. The real concern, an embarrassing one in a taboo area, might not have surfaced for a number of interviews. By being tentative at the beginning of the interview, the worker was able to get at the problem behind the problem.

Supervision approaches. Supervisors can help students become more conscious of the importance of sessional contracting by concentrating on the tentative beginnings of their contracts as they discuss their practice. Asking the client what he or she was working on can help students see that particular interviews or sessions with clients moved on too quickly, without adequate exploration. Often real concerns emerge near the end of the session, in what has been described as the doorknob therapy phenomenon. By examining the conversation at the beginning of a session, it is often possible to pick up the cues to concerns that will emerge later.

The supervision process can be an important demonstration of the skill of sessional contracting. Students will often bring partial or incomplete concerns to the attention of their supervisors, who can employ the same tentativeness in their discussions with the students. The following excerpt is an example:

Fred came into my office appearing agitated and somewhat upset. He asked if I had a minute for an interpretation of a policy question. I said, "Sure, what is it?" He described a problem related to agency policy and eligibility for service in respect to a specific client. I interpreted the policy as I understood it, and he nodded his head vigorously, agreeing with me. He then went on to describe an interview he had just had with a client in which the client had been abusive in response to Fred's interpretation of the policy and had attacked him and the agency. I said I thought that was upsetting and wondered if he wanted to spend a minute talking about it. He said he did, because he hadn't really known how to handle it and wasn't feeling too good about what had happened.

Supervisors who are themselves busy and under pressure may find it easiest to deal with only the first issue presented, even though they sense there might be more behind it. As has been noted, some supervisors are concerned that if they invite the student to explore an issue in greater depth, the student might accept the invitation. Certainly, there are times when it is necessary to put off discussion until both the student and the supervisor can devote adequate attention to a problem. Often, it is impossible to examine details on every issue. In any case, if an issue is not dealt with the first time it comes up, it could emerge again and thus provide a second opportunity to deal with it.

Elaboration Skills

Workers' skills that are helpful in encouraging clients to tell their stories include containment, questioning, focused listening, reaching inside silences, and moving from the general to the specific. In direct practice, *containment* helps the worker to resist the tendency to provide a solution or an answer to a client's problem before the client has elaborated it in some detail. The feeling many workers have that they are effective only if they can solve their clients' problems can lead them to propose answers—before they really understand the questions.

As clients describe their concerns, they should be led to provide details with *questioning*, such as "Could you tell me a little more about that?" Often the worker has a hard time understanding why a client has brought up a particular issue; it may seem to be idle chatter, irrelevant to their meeting. *Focused listening* encourages the worker to listen with the working contract in mind in order to discover clues to the real meaning of a conversation.

Although silences are key moments in practice, it may be difficult for workers to understand their meaning. They could experience discomfort during silence and try to change the subject. Observation of videotapes of the practice of 11 workers indicated that over 60% of the time, the discussion following a silence moved away from the client's concern (Shulman, 1992). If workers understand that silences are a form of conversation, they can wait the silences out and ask why clients have become silent. If workers have a hunch, they can *reach inside the silences* and try to articulate the feelings. This often frees the client to make a next move.

The skill of *moving from the general to the specific* is very important in practice in helping professions. The client may begin an interview by raising a general problem, such as: "It's getting awfully tough these days to raise teenagers, with drugs and the way morals are changing." If the worker begins a general discussion of the problems of raising teenagers, the client's real concern may be missed. Underlying most general comments by clients, there is very specific concern. Workers have a better chance of getting at the concern by reaching for the specific with a question such as, "Have you had trouble with your daughter this week?" The general problem of raising teenagers may quickly become that of a specific problem a client is having with her daughter.

Requesting elaboration of the specifics of the problem is also helpful. Note in the following example how the worker helped the client to provide details of the concern:

> Mrs. Fredericks told me she found it very hard dealing with her teenage foster daughter. I asked if there recently had been a specific example. She said there was and described how the daughter had come in at 3:00 A.M. earlier that week, and Mrs. Fredericks had no idea where she was. I said I thought that must have been pretty upsetting for her. She said it was. I asked what happened when the daughter came in. She told me that she had gotten very angry and ended up getting into a fight with her. I asked if she could tell me about a bit of the conversation with her daughter. I said that if we could take a look at what happened, I might be able to help her think through what to do when it happens again.

Supervision approaches. In modeling the skills of elaboration, supervisors can help students understand their functional role, as well as how to deal with their feelings about the work. The tendency of students to try to offer solutions because they believe that is how a worker helps has been noted; often they see the worker as someone who "has the answers." The model of practice in their minds is that clients tell them their problems, and workers come up with the solutions. Because life is not that simple and solutions are often hard to find, students are frequently disappointed at not being able to help enough. After warning of the temptation to intervene precipitately, the supervisor can open up a discussion of the student's sense of the helping role with a question such as, Exactly *how* do you see yourself giving help? When students feel less responsible for providing instant solutions, they can allow clients more time to elaborate.

To help students develop the skill of dealing with silences, the supervisor can ask about their feelings during a silence. Often students seem to regard a silence as negative feedback on their work. This is true in some cases, and supervisors need to help students develop the confidence to reach for such feedback from clients. More often, however, silence is not negative feedback at all. The supervisor can ask students to speculate on what a silence might mean. As the students become more aware of how silences affect them, they will develop self-confidence and begin to reach inside the silences.

The supervisory relationship exemplifies to students the skills of elaboration, particularly the skill of moving from the general to the specific. As in client relationships, the most common problem in supervision is the tendency to deal with generalities. Behind a general question raised by a student is often a specific troubling incident. It takes only a few minutes of the supervisor's time to ask the student to describe what happened, and when the student reports what the client said, to ask, And how did you respond? The supervisor must let the student know that the details of the interaction are needed in order to think through the problem. A case conference in which the discussion centers only on the client, focusing on the diagnosis and treatment plan, can leave the student at a loss. Instead, the discussion should center on the interaction between the student and the client. It is from the specifics of the interaction that an understanding of the situation and a plan for action will emerge.

The following example is a report of a supervisor's discussion with a student of her initial interviews with a client. The discussion remained at a general level and was of limited help. The student, Nancy, raises concerns about her interview with a young, hospitalized client who is considering an abortion. She is also concerned about how to handle procedures with other professionals with whom she has consulted on the case. In this initial student-supervisor conference, the discussion went as follows:

> NANCY: As I was saying, I don't have anything great to say today.
> SUPERVISOR: Oh, everything you say is great, Nancy.
> NANCY: (Laughing.) Right. I had two sessions with this young girl named Fran in the clinic last week. One each day. And I consultated—is that how you say it?
> SUPERVISOR: Consulted.
> NANCY: (Laughs.) *Consulted* with two colleagues, Risa and Frank, about this girl, in between the sessions. She was having an abortion. I suppose you might call it abortion counseling, seeing if that's what she really wanted.
> There were some problems with her family. Her mother was supposedly very much against it. She's living in the home. Her parents are taking on a lot of stuff. Anyway, I guess the only thing I did about that is, I went back the next day. I came back here, and I was thinking that it was all quite clear. What I had tried to do—although it just kind of emerged out of the interview—was just to try to get it all out and look at it with her and then get her to look at what each issue was.
> SUPERVISOR: I hear you.
> NANCY: You know, the abortion, what it meant, and what was happening at home, I guess. When I came back, I asked Risa a little bit about why the parents were upset,

and then Risa got into it about the seriousness of the whole matter. It just seemed that what she was saying was that this was awesome for somebody to be considering. And it struck me that I didn't think so, and then I talked to Frank, and he said the same thing. I'm beginning to think that there's something wrong with my conception (laughs) of how I see problems. And he was saying there's a lot of dynamics there, and you have to sort out all of these different things.

SUPERVISOR: I guess I'm sort of wondering, what stage was she at?

NANCY: I think I sort of look at it quite simply, like I don't want to go into all that stuff right away. She was quite clear about what she wanted to do.

SUPERVISOR: I mean, how far along was she?

NANCY: Oh, seven weeks. She'd been in for an operation, and they found out that she was pregnant too . . . . So there was a . . . there were an awful lot of complications.

SUPERVISOR: Why do you think that their views are so different—Risa's and Frank's and yours?

NANCY: (Laughing.) Well, I guess, the negative part of me thinks, "These workers, they just have to be so professional that they really need something to do."

SUPERVISOR: You mean, Risa and Frank are creating a mountain out of a molehill?

NANCY: Yeah, exactly. And then the other part of me thinks, "Gee, you know, there must be something I'm missing." I can see that there are some things that have to be ironed out and looked at, but it just didn't strike me as being such a big deal.

SUPERVISOR: I've worked with some people in this area, and it can be a big thing and it cannot be a big thing. I guess my sense of it is, how does the girl view the abortion? Does she see it as murder? Which is what some people with antiabortion views might say.

NANCY: No, no.

SUPERVISOR: Or does she see it almost as a birth control kind of a measure?

NANCY: Well, as more like a birth control thing. She just felt that she just wasn't ready to have a child.

The conversation continued in a general vein, moving back and forth between the client's perception of the problem and Nancy's continued concern about the other professionals' opinions. At no point, however, did the supervisor ask her to describe, in some detail, how the interviews with the client had proceeded. Nancy persisted during the conference in emphasizing her inability to see why the abortion would be such a big deal.

Note the differences between this general discussion and the following excerpts from a conference between the same student and supervisor about another client held just one week later. In this situation, Nancy feels that the client, who is in a hospital, is avoiding talking about a number of real issues related to her discharge. For the student, the issue is similar to the one with her previous client: What is my role, and how do I reach for possible underlying issues and feelings? This time, quickly moving to reconstruct the interview by employing role play, the supervisor helped Nancy explore the question more productively.

SUPERVISOR: Okay, anything else about Louise?

NANCY: Well, I guess I kind of know what to do with that, but I wonder, because her (the client) thing is that everything's gotta be okay, because she can't face pain very well. And when I'm there, often she'll say, "Everything was really terrible a week ago or a few days ago, but everything's just fine now, I'm just living blissed out . . . . Everything's just great, and it's going to be good when I go home, it's just going to be fine."

SUPERVISOR: And this happens every time you come?

NANCY: Yeah.

SUPERVISOR: Maybe you ought to talk about that.

NANCY: I said to her this morning, "You probably feel okay now, right at the moment, but there must be a lot of hurt and a lot of pain, or you wouldn't have gone through all that stuff." I was trying to get back to the pain, but I'm just not sure where to go with that.

SUPERVISOR: How does she answer when you say that?

NANCY: She won't get into it.

SUPERVISOR: What are you feeling at the time, when that's happening?

NANCY: I'm feeling like this is getting into a social visit, and I'm just not sure what my role is here. I almost feel like a candy striper instead of a social worker. And I just don't know how much I should try to therapize or just listen or . . . . I don't want to interfere, but I don't want to be completely useless, either.

SUPERVISOR: Your feeling, your gut feeling is that she tried to turn it into a social visit. And I'm wondering what your sense is, going on that feeling, what she might be trying to accomplish.

NANCY: She's just avoiding, I think, and trying to make it all seem nice, when— and afraid of the real feelings and on the verge of tears. Afraid of expressing the feelings. Afraid of the pain, afraid of breaking down, or whatever.

SUPERVISOR: She has a good pattern of avoidance. Her whole family does that. Do you want to try that interview again with me? I'll play Louise . . . .

NANCY: And you're saying how nice it is now, everything's just fine.

SUPERVISOR: (Role playing.) I really had a bad time, but I'm feeling really good now. It's going to be okay when I get home.

NANCY: How do you know it's going to be okay when you get home?

SUPERVISOR: Well, I can really feel it's going to be okay. I just know, 'cause it was really bad before, and I think I know what to do now. It's really going to be good now.

NANCY: Well, I kind of . . . .

SUPERVISOR: But I still want to see you.

NANCY: Yeah, I feel, I guess I should just say, "I don't think we're getting anywhere the way we're talking." Because you're coming across like everything's fine, but I can sense a lot of pain in you—you're almost crying right now, and yet you're saying everything's just great. How are you really feeling?

SUPERVISOR: You know what that does for me. I feel really scared.

NANCY: How?

SUPERVISOR: Like you hit me.

NANCY: Oh dear.

SUPERVISOR: No, it's good.

NANCY: Is it?

SUPERVISOR: Yeah.

NANCY: I thought it was too heavy.

SUPERVISOR: No, I mean, it was heavy, but I'm not sure what I'm going to do with it, being Louise. I don't know Louise that well, but I feel you really connected with me. Have you talked to Louise that way?

NANCY: I came close to it today, and I just didn't think . . . . I wanted to talk to you about it, because I just didn't know what my role was there.

SUPERVISOR: I felt really good. You saw my tears, you acknowledged them—and even more—my pain. You refused to believe me and called it the way it was. Part of me was scared to death, but part of me really liked it. I guess, up to now, you have also been avoiding.

NANCY: I think I have been.

SUPERVISOR: You're avoiding, like she's avoiding.

NANCY: I think I was, and I don't know what my role is, because I'm afraid I won't know what to do. I think I'd better clarify exactly what my role is, and then I'll feel more comfortable.

SUPERVISOR: That avoidance thing is deadly.

NANCY: Yeah, I really let it go this morning.

SUPERVISOR: So, how did that feel, trying that out?

NANCY: It felt a lot better. It felt a lot more real to me, because I was beginning to feel like, like a visitor. (Laughs.) Which is . . . .

SUPERVISOR: I've been in that spot before, it's an easy spot to get into. When we're working with people and confronted with their problems, because their problems seem so overwhelming and we feel inadequate, it's easy for us to avoid them. I don't know where to go with this girl. You know, obviously, she has really deep problems. All these psychiatrists have been poking around at her, and nobody knows the answer.

This brief excerpt shows how Nancy began to face the issues of clarity of role, denial on the part of the client, and some of her own feelings that made it difficult for her to reach behind the facade of denial and to demand real work. (*See the following section*). In a sense, the supervisor modeled the demand by reaching behind the general discussion of clients and the student's own denial ("everything seems to be going all right") and getting into the specific details of the work. Thus, effective teaching by supervisors involves a continuous moving between analysis of the specifics of the student's practice and the generalizations that emerge from that practice.

If a supervisor senses resistance to such a discussion, the student's feelings should be explored. The student may be unsure of the supervisor's intent or, in the past, may have had poor experiences with supervisors who might have been punitive in their comments. If the purpose of the discussion becomes clear and the supervisor is supportive rather than judgmental or harsh, the student may be more open to this kind of help. If resistance is still present, the supervisor must make a demand for work because discussion of the specifics of the interview is critical if help is to be offered. A supervisor who feels comfortable about offering this kind of help will find it easier to make this demand.

Making a Demand for Work

The notion of the demand for work is based on the assumption that clients feel some ambivalence about the work to be done. On the one hand, the client is reaching out to deal with life and solve problems, to take responsibility for actions; on the other, the client wants to avoid this necessity. A client may want to discuss painful feelings, for example, but at the same time may be afraid of them. This ambivalence results in a willingness to work as well as in resistance.

Resistance manifests itself in many forms: Clients may not return to the agency or may miss an appointment following a particularly difficult session, refuse to be serious about the work, or avoid dealing with difficult areas and feelings. Workers may report sessions that appear to be an illusion of work, lacking in substance and feeling. Apathy, acting out, and passive resistance are other ways clients resist moving into difficult areas. The important point for workers to understand is, however, that resistance is often a sign that the work is going well, rather than a sign that it is going badly. When ambivalence is clearly understood and resistance is seen as *part of the work*, they can recognize the importance of being prepared to make a demand for work on the client, rather than becoming discouraged and easing up.

When a positive relationship has been established within a clear contract and the worker has demonstrated a capacity for empathy and understanding of a client's feelings, then it is possible for the worker to make clear demands on the client to act in his or her own interests. The client may initially get angry at the worker's demand, but that is exactly what is needed from the worker. In all life situations, people who care about each other are willing to take risks by making demands on each other.

' Specific skills that workers can use in making a demand for work include partializing, holding to focus, challenging the illusion of work, and using facilitative confrontation. *Partializing* is used to help clients who present numerous problems with which they are having difficulty. It is often a way of saying, "Look, there's nothing

I can do." By breaking overwhelming problems into more manageable parts, the worker is, in effect, demanding work from the client. Then, when clients begin to work on one part of a problem, it is not unusual for them to switch from one concern to another as soon as the worker gets close. The skill of *holding to focus* entails asking clients to stay on a particular issue until it is resolved. The following example shows how a worker partialized a client's multiple problem and held the client to focus:

> It was our first session together. Mrs. Carter told me that her sixteen-year-old son had been suspended from school and had gotten into a fight with a neighbor. The neighbor had complained to the landlord, and now he was threatening to evict her. The neighbor had also come to see her and had been abusive and threatening. When she had talked to her son to try to get him to apologize, he had gotten angry and had stormed out of the house. She wasn't sure what to do about anything. I told her I could see it was an upsetting time for her. I pointed out she had to deal with the school, her landlord, her neighbor, and most difficult of all, her son. I said I thought it would help if we could take things one at a time. Where would she like to start? She said the landlord's threats were most frightening to her. I asked her to tell me about the conversation with the landlord.

By partializing this problem, the worker made it more manageable. As the conversation continued, however, the client shifted back to the school suspension, and the worker needed to hold the client to focus:

> Mrs. Carter said she couldn't promise the landlord her son would behave, because his being suspended from school and hanging around the house all the time led to trouble. She went on to talk about the call from the school principal. I asked if we could stick to the landlord for a moment, and then discuss the call with the principal. I could see they were connected problems, but it would help if we stayed with one problem at a time.

Another form of making a demand for work is the skill of *challenging the illusion of work*. A worker who finds sessions with a client boring and lacking in substance and feeling, and who believes that the client feels the same way, may sense that they are getting nowhere. By challenging the illusion of work, the worker can call attention to the pattern. It is important to make clear the point that *the client is not being accused of having created the illusion of work* and that *the worker is merely pointing it out to help both of them explore its meaning*. The worker might say, for example, "I've been thinking about our last few sessions. It seems to me the discussion has been superficial. We haven't gotten our teeth into anything important. I wonder if you have any ideas why that's so." Opening up the discussion in this way can encourage the client to suggest a reason why the discussion is difficult; the work may have entered a taboo area, such as sexual relations, for example. As the client discusses the difficulty of talking to the worker about sex, the work will turn from illusion to substance.

The skill of *facilitative confrontation* is illustrated in an example in the next section, in which a worker shares her anger in confronting Mark, a teenaged client who was making no effort on his own behalf at school. This was done effectively and in a facilitative manner only because a good working relationship had been developed. Used prematurely, the skill could be experienced by the client as evidence of the worker's harshness and lack of understanding. The proper blend of caring and demand is subtle and difficult to achieve. Workers are often either demanding *or* empathic; usually, they find it difficult to make an empathic demand. Because this problem extends to all human relationships, it is no wonder that it poses difficulty in the helping professions as well. Workers who are empathic and understanding can develop a good relationship with clients but are not necessarily helpful, while those who are just demanding are rejected by clients as being harsh. Workers who put the two together, however, appear to be most effective.

Supervision approaches. The supervisor's discussions of student practice often uncover moments when students would have felt like making a demand but were uncomfortable about it. Students describe being bored in an interview or upset because a client continues to make commitments but never follows them through. They have moments when they feel angry at a client but are afraid to let the client know because, students say, they fear taking too much responsibility for their client's lives.

By examining these moments and helping students understand the interplay between demand and caring, the supervisor can help students to trust their own instincts in most situations. It is not unprofessional to care whether a client makes it, and the client needs to know that the worker cares. One does not take away the right to self-determination by demanding that people act in their own self-interest. In fact, the client often desperately needs just such a demand in order to take the next step.

In discussions of the demand for work, students often reflect on the general difficulty of making demands in everyday life situations, as with friends, children, or spouses. Such discussions can be helpful if they focus on how this difficulty affects their practice with clients. One reason students may avoid making a demand is that they lack confidence in their ability to help. The student may say, in effect: "If I make a demand on a client, and he takes me up on it, then what will I do?" This is an indication to the supervisor of a need for help in developing and deepening the student's own work phase skills. It is also often a cue that the student is concerned about handling feelings.

As with the other practice skills, the supervisor can contribute by demonstrating the power of making a demand for work. Students may be very resistant, for example, about sharing their material with supervisors and other colleagues by the use of process recordings or videotapes. Their negative reactions to being asked to use these techniques often serve as covers for their fears about the unknown. By their resistance, students are waiting to see if the supervisor can be put off by their answer to the demand for work. The supervisor who recognizes this will empathize with students while making his or her expectations about the work clear.

One way supervisors can usefully apply their own work phase skills with students to illustrate a practice skill is by demonstrating the power of the demand for work on job management. Supervisors who set clear expectations about how students are to manage their agency responsibilities and who also are open to consider the realities of the situation help students become more responsible. Making a demand for work is also especially helpful when a student is in personal trouble. Supervisors must be empathic about the strains faced by students who are experiencing personal problems and also be sensitive to the effects these can have on their work. In these situations, supervisors can often be helpful in referring students for outside help. However, it is not helpful to stop making expectations of students or to try to cover for a student who is having a hard time. It is better for the supervisor to maintain expectations about the work and thus help troubled students to function effectively in the agency, which, in turn, can help them deal with their personal problems—and ultimately those of the client.

The following example, in which a supervisor requests a student to share the details of his practice with process recordings, illustrates the demand for work coupled with empathy:

> I told Frank that I was expecting to get some of his material on his first interview, so we could discuss how he began. I hadn't received it and wondered why. Frank said he had been very busy that week. I told him I realized the load was heavy, but I thought he would have had time to dictate some notes on that interview. He paused and then said that he wasn't sure why it was necessary to do that. Frank had stiffened and looked quite defensive at that point.
>
> I told him that I had sensed that there might be some reluctance on his part to do it and that perhaps this would be a good time to discuss it. I asked why he felt it wasn't necessary. He said he couldn't see the purpose, and anyway he didn't think he could remember what went on at the sessions. I said that developing the skill of recall was a difficult one. I asked if he had ever written anything like this before. He said he had not. I told him perhaps part of the problem was that I could have been more helpful in describing what it was I was asking for. I asked if he understood. He said he wasn't sure, so I explained that I did not want the whole interview but rather just some brief comments about the conversation in the beginning, a summary of how the interview went, some more detail about any parts he was interested in discussing, and how it ended. I told him I thought it wasn't easy as a new student to share his work with me, but I wanted to reassure him that I wasn't asking in order just to snoop, or to be critical. I felt that if I had some of the detail of what he was saying and doing with his clients, I might be more helpful to him.
>
> I asked him if it was true that he had been concerned about what I would do with the records. He said he was, and that he felt that the first interview hadn't gone very well at all. He was embarrassed to present it. I told him that I didn't expect these interviews to go perfectly and that I thought by going over some of his work with clients I might be able to help him identify what he did that went well, as well as what he could do better. I then asked if he could first recreate from memory some of the details of this first interview and then would try to show what I meant. I said I was willing to work from his memory of the experience, this time, but that the next time I would be expecting a written record.

It was important for the supervisor to explore the student's feelings about using the recorded material, while, at the same time, making it quite clear that the material was expected.

There would be a slightly different problem in encouraging use of process recordings by experienced students, who may not have had such experiences or training in their previous practice. Such students may feel they are expected to know more than they really do, and they are embarrassed about sharing their uncertainties with their supervisors. A problem also arises if recordings have been used in a punitive manner. If recordings are used to draw mistakes to students' attention routinely, with no demonstration of empathy or support, they may give the idea that workers are expected to be perfect. An experience such as this can become a block to any future use of the technique. A supervisor who uses recordings to explore past experiences with students and then tries to help them sort out how they could have done better frees the worker to take chances. In any case, students should be expected to meet the demand for work, in spite of their past experiences.

An important element in making the demand for work is that the helping person—worker or supervisor—assure the client or student of the helping person's confidence in his or her ability to take the next step. In general, people do not want others to give up on them. Even if a worker were to appear to be asking a supervisor to back off, the worker will often be disappointed if the supervisor does so.

Some supervisors fear that if they ask students to provide details or evidence of their work, the supervisor will be then expected to help with it. Because supervisors often are still learning with their right hand while teaching with their left, some uncertainty should be expected. When the supervisor's uncertainty is matched by that of the student, however, the result can be an illusion of work.

Sharing Own Feelings

In their interactions with clients, workers experience many normal emotions. Nevertheless, in some models of the helping professions, the expression of one's own feelings while working with clients is considered to be unprofessional. According to the practice theory developed by Schwartz (1961), however, this forces an artificial dichotomy between the personal and the professional. Rather, he maintains, feelings can be used professionally, as long as they are related to the worker's function and to the purpose of the encounter. Workers can—and should—spontaneously share such feelings as frustration, anger, and caring for clients. Clients find it easier to trust such a worker, whom they describe as being a *real* person.

Workers must seek to develop the same capacity to express feelings that they expect of their clients, as well as the ability to express their feelings spontaneously. As workers deepen their understanding of their function, they will learn to avoid making such mistakes as expressing feelings that are not helpful to clients. If a client comes on strong, for example, expressing concerns by making an angry attack on the worker, the worker needs to respond honestly at the moment, by openly expressing his or her feelings. With experience, however, workers develop the ability to see past the anger and to understand the hurt that is underneath; this makes them see that a better response might be to reach for that hurt. This ability will never be acquired, however, if workers are constantly monitoring their own feelings and are afraid to take risks. If they make mistakes, they can always apologize later. Clients are more accepting of those workers who are honest and apologetic when they make a mistake than they are of those who appear to be paragons of virtue—always cool, objective, and composed.

In the following example, the worker's expression of feeling was critical. The example is drawn from the ending phase of work with an adolescent about to leave the care of the agency. Mary had known the worker for two years, and an intimate relationship had developed. During the conversation the worker revealed her feeling about Mary, saying:

> "I was beginning to think about the fact that we only have a couple of more sessions together. To be honest with you, although I'm glad you're going to be able to move out on your own now and start to be independent, I'm going to miss you." There was a long silence, and I could sense that Mary was struggling for composure. She said, "You were the best worker I've ever had. I could always talk to you when I had things on my mind. I'm a little afraid about who I'm going to talk to now." The worker replied, "Can you say some more about what it was about me that you thought made me the best worker?"

By asking the client for the specific qualities that she found helpful, the worker can help her begin to think about the transition she will need to make to other support systems such as family or friends. If clients are aware of the qualities they had found helpful in the worker, they may be able to find others within the community with those same characteristics to substitute the role of the worker. An important conversation was taking place between the worker and the client about their parting; it might not have occurred if the worker had not openly expressed her own feelings.

Being open about feelings includes a willingness to share the anger and frustration workers often feel when they think a client is not trying. For example, after months of helping a client through a difficult school situation, a worker found out that Mark, the client, was again avoiding doing homework and was about to be suspended. The worker felt frustrated and angry at the waste of all her efforts. She told Mark:

> I want you to know I'm really mad that you are just ready to blow everything at school. We've put a lot of time and effort into this, getting you back in, sorting out the problems you had with your teacher. Things were starting to straighten out, but now, you seem willing to just let your life get screwed up. Damn it all, that makes me mad and frustrated.

Mark responded with anger and said that it was not any of the worker's business. It was his own life, and he would do with it as he wished. The interview ended on this note. At the next session, however, Mark reported that he had seen the teacher, had gone over the missed assignments, and had worked out a plan for what he had to do to catch up. The demand, the anger, the frustration, all of which represented real caring on the part of the worker, were critical in helping this client take a next step on his own behalf.

Supervision approaches. A review of client interviews is a helpful way to teach the skill of sharing feelings. Inquiring what students felt at particular moments when the supervisor thinks they might have been upset or angry, for example, can encourage them to share these feelings. Supervisors may also share their thoughts about spontaneity and sharing feelings, not just in practice but in everyday life. This provides an opportunity for the supervisor to empathize with the difficulty of sharing feelings, while pointing out how it might have helped in a particular instance. The supervisor might say, for example, "If you had leveled with the client right at that moment, how do you think she might have reacted?" In thinking about how the client would have responded, it often becomes clear that leveling could have brought a positive reaction.

Students often respond to an exercise such as this with a comment like: "It seems so simple, and I don't know why I don't do it." This opens up discussion of the difficulties of sharing feelings in our society and provides an opportunity to point out how the worker can be simultaneously professional and personal. Most importantly, the supervisor can use the exercise to give the student permission to make mistakes. I often suggest to a student who has made a mistake when being spontaneous with a client that it was a *good* mistake. It was good because the student was honest, and it was a mistake because it was not directly related to the current concerns of the client, or perhaps there was a better way of dealing with the client's problem. When the supervisor believes in the importance of spontaneity, learning is seen as a process in which the student makes mistakes, analyzes them, learns from the analysis, then goes back and corrects the mistake, and moves on to make more sophisticated mistakes. This provides a sense of freedom that allows students to explore their own skills in this area.

The skills in sharing one's own feelings are easiest to teach when they are actively modeled. Anger, a common reaction in human relationships, is one of the feelings we are usually taught to suppress. When supervisors are angry with students, it is a mistake to hide the anger while expressing it in a manner considered to be more professional instead of being honest about it. Professional anger is usually less direct, colder, and more hurtful than real anger. Students who find, perhaps after some time, that they can have a positive relationship with their supervisors, which includes caring as well as anger, and that getting angry does not destroy a relationship, are freed to experiment in the same way with clients.

Sharing Data

Another important skill factor for workers is the ability to share data with clients in a meaningful way. In this sense, data include information, facts, as well as the values and beliefs held by the worker that may be relevant and helpful to the client in a particular instance. This is an area of much confusion in the helping professions; workers may consider it improper to provide data to clients because they should figure things out for themselves. Clients may want access to the worker's data but do not want it imposed on them as if it were the only truth. Workers who realize that their knowledge, beliefs, and values are only one part of reality are able to make them available to clients without feeling the need to convince them.

The notion of presenting ideas as open to challenge runs contrary to many views about how people help. Workers have become so used to being sold on ideas that they may believe they are only effective if they can sell their ideas to their clients. On the contrary, workers are more effective when they make their ideas available rather than try to impose them. Clients will use information or values or beliefs only when they perceive and appreciate their importance. In fact, they may reject ideas they feel are being sold to them by the worker. If information is shared at a time when it is not relevant to the client, it will not be used. Workers who suggest that a client needs to know something in an area that is unrelated to the client's sense of urgency will be perceived as pursuing their own interests.

Workers should feel free to share their ideas directly. Trying to lead the client to answer, as by asking questions that will get the client to give the answer the worker wants, often shifts the work away from the client's task. Instead of working on the problem, the client attempts to decipher what it is the worker wants. Workers thus should make their data available directly, ensuring that they are related to the client's urgency, leaving the client free to use or to reject the ideas.

The following excerpt is from the records of a worker who was asked for her opinion by a young unmarried mother faced with a decision whether to keep her child:

> I explained to Dora that she was asking a tough question. In the last analysis, she was going to have to make that decision, and only *she* really knew whether she could keep the baby or not. I asked her why she was asking me at this point, what was troubling her. She went on to tell me, on the one hand, a part of her wanted to keep the baby, but she was afraid that she was so young she would have nothing left of her life if she did. On the other, she kept thinking of what it would be like if she gave the baby up and felt guilty for not being more responsible.
>
> I acknowledged some of those feelings, telling her it was not unusual to feel both simultaneously. I told her it was a tough decision, because no matter which way she went it was going to hurt. I then went on to say that, from the agency's point of view,

there was no indication that she would be an unfit mother. Therefore, the choice was really up to her. From getting to know her over these weeks, however, I had the sense that the biggest part of her really wanted to have more time to experience life. If this were true, she probably would be better off in the long run if she placed the child than if she tried to keep it because she felt guilty.

I paused, and there was silence. I said, "I've just told you how I felt, but I don't think that really helps very much. In the end, it still has to be your decision because you have to live with it." She nodded, and said she knew that was true. She then went on to say that it helped for her to take in other points of view and that she really had wanted to know how I saw things.

Supervision approaches. By exploring students' feelings of responsibility for providing data, the supervisor can be helped in sorting out the differences between their opinions and reality. When the supervisor sees that they are trying to sell their ideas to clients, it is often possible to identify clients' resistance and to demonstrate that clients cannot be easily "changed." When the supervisor senses that students are holding back, it is helpful to explore their mixed feelings about giving advice and sharing their own views.

Practice research findings have indicated that better working relationships may be developed by workers who freely offer their own ideas to clients and then leave them open to rejection (Shulman, 1978). Students can be helped to understand this from their own experience with the supervisor. Asking how students would feel if the supervisor had some information they needed but held it back so that they might learn it for themselves, for example, can help them understand clients' similar feelings.

Skills in sharing data are most closely related to the educational function. The supervisor has to recognize that students, like clients, must learn by themselves; they have to develop their own ideas and insights as they go along. Even ideas that most supervisors are very clear about have to be learned anew by students, and time must be allowed for them to assimilate ideas that supervisors have developed over a period of years. Supervisors can serve as guides along the way, and if their views are qualified and shared in an undogmatic way, workers will find them helpful.

Sometimes a supervisor suspects that a student accepts too easily whatever the supervisor says. In such a case, a discussion of the authority theme is in order. Helping students to keep the supervisor's views in perspective and to use her or him as a resource for the student's own learning is a part of the supervision process.

Dealing With Endings and Transitions

The dynamics of the ending of the supervisor-student relationship are quite similar to those of the worker-client ending (Shulman, 1992). The parallel nature of these processes can provide the supervisor with an opportunity to demonstrate the very skills the student needs to employ with his or her clients.

The context of the ending will, of course, vary considerably. The student may be leaving either voluntarily or involuntarily, or the supervisor may feel a great sense of loss or of relief when a particular student leaves. Still, some common themes persist such as denial of the feelings associated with the student's leaving. As the date approaches, limited discussion of the event takes place. Those who are leaving may come in on weekends to clean out their desks, so that they never actually have to say good-bye—*not* because they do not care about the supervisor or other staff members, but because they care too much.

A sense of urgency about unfinished business is also characteristic. Both the student and the supervisor have much to say to each other, sharing positive or negative feelings, or both. Even if the relationship has been a poor one, a constructive discussion of the reasons why the supervisor and the student had difficulty dealing with each other can be extremely helpful. In the "farewell bouquet" ending, students have some final thoughts about the experience they would like to share. The "bouquets" may be positive, or alternatively, all of the previously unstated negatives may finally emerge. Many agencies require final, or exit, interviews, in which students can share thoughts and feelings that may have been difficult to express while they were at the agency.

Feelings of guilt may also be characteristic of a student's ending experiences. Could the student have put more into the experience and gotten more out of it? Should the supervisor have been more available? It is not uncommon to detect a period of mourning as the ending approaches. Apathy in conferences, for example, may signal strong feelings about leaving. At the same time, there may be very positive feelings about making a new beginning. Students, for example, may be starting their professional careers, ready to test themselves in the real world. The supervisor may be able to help them with any feelings of ambivalence they have about facing the challenge.

Both the supervisor and the student may be inclined to be overly positive about the ending experience. If they give in to the temptation to deal only with the positives, however, they will cut off an opportunity to use the ending phase effectively. Negatives expressed through anger and regression are also common in this phase; for example, students may return to patterns of work or relationships that marked their early days at the agency. If students have become close to other staff members and if the atmosphere has been supportive and intimate, colleagues also may experience some real sense of rejection, coupled with feelings of loss.

Supervision approaches. One of the crucial reasons supervisors must devote careful attention to the student ending experience is that a student who is leaving is probably having similar experiences with clients. If the student's feelings about the endings are not dealt with, this can adversely affect the effectiveness of agency services. A number of procedures can be used by supervisors to make an ending a helpful experience for the student.

First, the supervisor can call attention to the approach of an ending by noting the date at a conference or a staff meeting. This sets the ending phase in motion.

Second, the supervisor can call attention to the dynamics of the ending as they emerge. If the supervisor notices apathy in conferences, for example, a direct question can be used to examine whether it has something to do with the student's ending experience.

Third and most importantly, the supervisor can level with his or her own feelings about the student's departure. Because it is hard to express feelings of warmth and closeness in any situation, the supervisor must take the first step. When these feelings are shared openly, they often provide the catalyst needed to help the student discuss similar emotions.

Fourth, the supervisor can structure an ending evaluation period that includes systematic attention to the supervision experience. The strengths of the relationship, as well as the weaknesses should be specifically identified. A summary of the learning that has occurred and an identification of a future learning agenda can help. Because of the tendency to be overly positive about the experience, the supervisor will have to reach hard for negatives and to be honest in sharing them with the student.

Fifth, attention to the ending between the student and other staff members is often appreciated. It is just as important for the supervisor to pay attention to the separation process when a student leaves, as it is to deal with the engagement process when a student joins the staff. Making announcements at staff meetings, briefly discussing the student's contributions, and reaching for the feelings of other staff members, as well as sharing one's own feelings, can all go far to help the staff deal directly with the loss of a colleague. If the students are not assisted in this way, the ending is often no more than a "farewell party," in which a limited exchange of real meaning is made and the staff is left with the feeling of unfinished business.

Finally, the supervisor can use the experience to help the student focus on the specific skills of dealing with client endings. By identifying what is happening in their own relationship as well as the parallel process with the client, the supervisor can contribute to the student's ability to deal with the often neglected termination phase of practice.

The following report of how a supervisor dealt with a student's ending at a family agency illustrates a number of the dynamics of workers' endings. The supervisor and the student had been together for one year, and the beginning of their work on endings was intermingled with his efforts to help her deal with termination with clients. The supervisor's report began:

> PREPARATORY WORK: In working with Fran (the student) on her practice with Terry (the client), it was apparent that she was most concerned about the coming ending. Fran had only three weeks left on her placement, and I felt it was time to focus on her ending work with Terry. Fran had been working with Terry for five months, and it was not certain whether Terry would want to continue counseling with another worker or terminate with the agency when Fran left.
>
> In a conference during which we discussed Terry, we did not go into great detail in discussing the skills needed to make the endings a useful piece of work. On her own, Fran had made a list of the issues that she and Terry had tackled together that Fran wanted to review with Terry. I mentioned that she and Terry had developed a relationship over time and that there would be some feelings about the coming ending. I suggested that perhaps Terry might feel angry or sad about the ending and that Fran should try to pull for these feelings in the session. Fran agreed that this would be important. I also stated the endings can be a difficult piece of work, because the therapist often has strong feelings about the endings as well. I pointed out that you are in a session dealing with your own feelings as well as the client's. Fran thought this might be true. She agreed to tape the session for our discussion at our next conference.

In this case, as all too often happens, the supervisor discussed the ending in relation to the client but ignored it in relation to the worker. The discussion of the dynamics of the worker-client process will remain lifeless as long as the dynamics of the supervisor-worker relationship are ignored. After studying endings, Fran could agree intellectually about what needs to be done, but emotionally she was not in touch with what was happening. Even though the supervisor described what it would be like for the worker to deal with her own feelings and the client's, unless he modeled how to do this in their session, the worker would respond to his actions, not his words. In the supervision conference that followed, the supervisor caught this mistake and moved into both endings with feelings.

SUPERVISION SESSION: I asked her how it went. Fran said that it was okay and then, immediately, that it was terrible. She was obviously upset. Fran then proceeded to summarize her session with Terry. They had talked about the various areas of Terry's life that had improved since coming for counseling. Terry summed up the improvement by saying that she felt a lot more confident and less pressure. She attributed this to the fact that she and Fran had done a lot of work on her self-esteem and that it had really improved significantly. Terry said she was able to break her high-low cycle and live a more balanced life.

Fran said it was at this point that she raised the issue of ending the counseling with Terry, because Terry was doing so well. Fran said she tried to reach for Terry's feelings about the ending but simply could not do it. She found it to be very difficult and pulled back. Fran began to cry when describing the process. The end result had been an agreement for Terry to call Fran when she returned from a short trip to discuss whether she needed another session.

I empathized with Fran, saying this was the hard part of the work, especially because she was feeling sad about the ending—as sad as Terry. Fran said that she did not want to cry with Terry. I asked her what held her back. She said that she did not like people seeing her cry. I asked if she felt that being a worker made it more difficult for her to cry. Fran felt there was some of that happening, but mostly, it was that she did not like to cry in front of people. I then talked about a theme we had discussed before, that when working with a client a counselor was both a professional and a real person and that at times it was very appropriate to react from your feelings about the work and the person. I continued that, with Terry, it would have been fine to say how much you would miss her, that you were feeling sad, and that the two of you could have cried together. Fran agreed that it would not have been so terrible.

At this point, I picked up the theme of endings for Fran. I said that she was not only ending with her clients, which was hard, but also that she was ending her stay at the agency. She had made a lot of friends here, and soon she would be ending with each of them. I told her I thought that must be hard for her. She agreed and began to cry. I then said that our relationship was also ending soon and that I would miss her. She agreed and said that she had a fine time here. At this point, there was a pause.

It is important that the supervisor move to return to the discussion about the ending with the client. This represents another example of dealing with the student's feelings in the process of supervision.

We then returned to talk about Terry. Fran wondered if she could do something more, like call her back, because she would like to have said more to her. She said she regretted not saying some of the things we talked about. I asked some more questions about how close she felt to Terry and suggested she could say some of what she felt about the ending when Terry called her. She agreed.

I suggested we listen to the tape. Fran resisted a bit, saying it was painful to listen to the session. What emerged from the tape was that Fran did a fine job with summarizing her work, and it was clear that Terry was ready to end the counseling relationship. It was also clear that Fran had many openings to talk about their feelings in relation to ending but had passed them up.

I talked about some of the endings skills, suggesting that one way to pull for feelings was first to talk about her own. We also discussed Fran's other clients who may feel somewhat differently about ending. For Terry, it was a natural ending of counseling, but others might want to continue and feel a bit angry at Fran's leaving in the middle. We did some tuning in about her other cases.

Fran felt that Jake (another client) was mad, and in fact, had been coming late to their appointments. Jake and his wife had been more aggressive in the last few sessions, for example, questioning closely what happened when I listened to Fran's audio tapes of their sessions with them. I suggested that perhaps Fran's hunch was right and that some of their behavior was related to the ending dynamics. She thought she should confront them directly. I agreed, and we role-played a number of ways she might get into this discussion. I suggested that there would be some sadness as well as anger, and Fran asked if I had any ideas about how to reach for it. I role-played as follows: 'I know you're feeling kind of frustrated with this situation about me leaving and your having to be transferred, but, you know, I'm also feeling sad about it. I'll miss you both, and I was wondering if you might be feeling some of the same.' I asked how it sounded to her, and she said fine. I said it was going to be hard. She agreed, but felt it would probably be easier than ending with Terry.

We then went on to discuss our coming evaluation and how we would handle supervision in the next few weeks.

SKILLS FOR PRACTICE WITH DIVERSE POPULATIONS

A number of issues need to be dealt with in helping students to develop the skills for practicing with diverse populations. The term *diverse populations* is used broadly here to include almost any client who is identifiable because of individual or social differences in race, ethnicity, gender, religion, sexual orientation, and so forth. First, students need to recognize the impact of working with someone who is different than themselves. For example, in the author's recent study of child welfare (Shulman, 1991), the worker's awareness of the potential impact of race when working with a Native American family was positively associated with the client's perception of the development of a working relationship and effective outcomes.

Second, students need to develop the skills (and courage) to address issues of difference when they emerge in the relationship. Courage is stressed because issues of difference, such as race, are taboo in our society and very difficult to deal with directly. When the author leads workshops for experienced professionals and inquires as to why subjects such as race are hard to discuss, participants share many reasons. One African-American social worker indicated that her "antennae were always up for possible racist comments." As a result, she continued, she needed to guard against the possibility of hearing racism even when it was not there. The author pointed out that given the experience of persons of color, it made a great deal of sense to be on guard and that she was describing an understandable defense. A white worker immediately responded: "That's it, that's the problem for me. I'm afraid to even talk about the issue because I may make a mistake, be misinterpreted, or perhaps let my personal bias or stereotypical perceptions slip out. When I sense we are getting into this area in my agency, it feels like walking on eggshells. I think I find it safer to just keep quiet than to risk being accused of being racist!" Another African-American participant pointed out that when white workers keep quiet, she often wonders if they are holding back because they are racist. The author pointed out the potential for significant miscommunication resulting from the taboo against open communication. He also suggested that if staff could not talk to each other about these issues, it must also make it difficult to deal with clients. As will be seen later in this section, when supervision approaches to helping students with this area of growth are explored, a major factor will be whether in a gender or cross-racial or -cultural pairing the supervisor models the skills with the student.

Third, the student needs to develop an appreciation for the cultural differences associated with different population groups. In the author's child welfare study (Shulman, 1991), when Native American clients perceived that their social worker understood their families and culture, there was a strong positive association with the client's perception of a good working relationship and worker helpfulness. This association was also present with "hard" outcome measures, such as whether or not children went into foster care and how long they stayed in care.

Fourth, students need to develop the ability to deal with issues of diversity in a differential manner. A common mistake occurs, for example, when a student learns about a particular culture and then attempts to impose on a client a cultural stereotype that actually does not fit. Continuing with the example of the Native American, a common cultural descriptor of the client includes a tolerance for silence. The author has observed workers explaining a relatively passive Native client in terms of this stereotype, suggesting that Native clients don't talk much. When one Native client was asked about his silence when meeting with a white worker, he responded: "When you stay quiet with a white worker long enough they get so nervous they go 'natter, natter, natter'." The client's silence was a communication to the worker, and dismissing it as a cultural characteristic would be a mistake. In many ways, in the name of practicing with cultural sensitivity, well-meaning students may actually be relating to clients in a stereotypical fashion.

Finally, if students are to strengthen their ability to practice with diverse populations, they need to understand, accept, and take control of their own sexist, racist, homophobic, ageist, and so on, attitudes and stereotypes. Both in the classroom and field, instructors need to create conditions so that these views may be openly expressed rather than remaining submerged because they represent the "wrong" social work attitudes. Student attitudes manifested by comments that reflect racial stereotyping, for example, can be seen as an opportunity for the instructor to open up an important part of the learning agenda. The supervisor must be able to share his or her own feelings, including a rejection of the stereotype or misinformation about another population, while simultaneously crediting the student with having the courage to risk the idea. If we recognize that our students come from diverse backgrounds themselves and that a social work experience may be their first opportunity to confront the cultural biases they have integrated from their family and community, then such comments early in a student's educational experience can be seen as "handles" for work.

Even more difficult is the task of the student who brings to school a liberal point of view that rejects all of the "isms." For these students, who fiercely defend their neutrality around race, gender, and so on, the learning challenge will be to examine the subtle forms of these attitudes and feelings that are present in all of us. In fact, the student who openly expresses these views may, in some ways, be easier to work with than the student for whom these attitudes are suppressed.

In a personal example that the author often shares with students, he recalls the first day of a workshop presented for an agency whose primary client group was HIV-positive gay men. Practicing what he preached, before the session the author tuned in to issues he might face as a straight social work professor working with staff in an essentially gay agency. He was prepared to respond directly to indirect cues about being an "outsider." As he entered the building elevator, two male construction workers entered as well. When the elevator door opened, he was greeted by a large banner displaying the agency's name: AIDS ACTION COMMITTEE. His immediate emotional reaction was to want to turn to the two men in the elevator and say: "I'm not gay!" After all of his careful tuning in, his homophobic fear emerged to catch him off guard. Also, why was he assuming that these construction workers were straight? This assumption revealed a stereotypical perception of not only the attitude of construction workers toward gay men but also of the sexual orientation of this occupational group. The author shared this experience with the workshop participants at the start of the session, which led to an important discussion of the concerns of the gay and lesbian members of staff (about two thirds) over the author's outsider status. In addition, concerns about feeling like outsiders were shared by one third of the staff who were straight.

The important message to students on issues of practice with diverse populations is that we recognize that growing up in our society has instilled some "isms" in all of us and that our professional development involves a lifelong effort to identify and accept these realities, while ensuring that we do not allow them to negatively impact on our practice. In fact, as illustrated in this example, this understanding may serve to strengthen practice with diverse populations.

Illustration: A White Student with a Native-American Family

In the following report of a white worker assigned to a Native-American family in a criminal justice setting, a social work student illustrates many of the skills described in this section.[4] The report begins with a session with Jim, a 14-year-old Native youngster who has been placed on probation for minor criminal offenses.

I tuned into Jim's feelings and tried to put his feelings into words. Jim had a tough look on his face. He slid himself down into a chair, his knees up close to his chest as if to protect himself. I said, "You look angry as hell today." No response. I waited out his silence. He said with a tone devoid of affect that he had a big fight last night after Indian dancing and that it lasted until 4 A.M. I asked him if he'd got hurt (empathizing). He said no, he never gets hurt. He was drunk, anyway. I was lucky he was sober this afternoon. I said, "Alcohol dims the pain. A 14-year-old drunk is a sad story to me." He said he knew. Jim said he had also siphoned gas out of a car last night. I said, "It is a lot for one night. Are you trying to tell me how bad you can be?" Jim looked at me intently. I said that behind that tough facade I thought there was a lot of pain. His voice changed. With a defensive tone he said, "Pain about what?" I said, "Maybe it was painful to feel you have to act like a hellion to get attention. He giggled and said, "It's not funny." I said, "I agree, it's not funny, it hurts." He cocked his head down. I waited out his silence. He said suddenly, "Nothing ever hurts anymore. Nobody cares about me anymore." I said, "Are you talking about home?" (Recognizing his indirect communication.) He said simply, "Yeah."

I recognized his indirect communication and tried to help him go from general to specific concerns. Jim had enumerated all the "bad" behaviors he had got into in the past two weeks. I said it was the third weekend that he had asked me to give him hell. He said that if I didn't, nobody would. I asked him if that's what he wanted his parents to do. He said, "No, I want them to understand me." I said that I knew things were rough for everyone at home right now, and asked whether he could tell me what had taken place at home that hurt. He looked away and said in a low voice, "They called me a rotten Indian." The affect of pain was so strong that he could not elaborate on his feelings or the specific circumstances. I said, "It hurts a lot, doesn't it? I wish I could take the pain away from you."

I tried to share my feelings openly. Jim said that he was sick and tired of being called a dirty Indian at home. The affect was anger. I tried to reach for the specific but got nowhere. He said that all his parents talked about was "dirty Indians this, silly Indians that. Who do they think they are anyway?" I said, "It may hurt to hear the word *Indian* coming from your own parents as a curse word." He asked me if I thought he was a dirty Indian. I said, "No, you are Indian all right, but the two words together are a terrible combination." He said, "What about a silly Indian?" I reached for his indirect communication and said, "You're checking out to see if I'm prejudiced aren't you?" He said, "Yup." I told him that it was for him to judge. He then told me that he would be on probation for awhile. I said I knew. He said in a low voice, "I don't think you can understand." I said gently, "Do you feel you can't win? What I mean

---

[4] See also the author's text *The Skills of Helping Individuals, Families and Groups* (3rd ed.) (pp. 238–242), Itasca, IL: F.E. Peacock, 1992.

is you can't be right and you can't be Indian." (Putting the client's feelings into words.) He said suddenly, "I don't know what *Indian* means. How am I supposed to grow up okay?" I put my arms around him and told him that he was right—I wasn't sure I could understand fully what it means to grow up as an Indian, that his hurt was choking me up right now.

I tried to help Jim view his parents in new ways. Jim said that his parents put him through a grinder whenever he is home. I said that it sounds horrible and asked what he meant. (Reaching for elaboration.) He said that his parents hassle him about every little detail about what he does at night. I jokingly said, "It's not such a horrible grinder after all!" He laughed. He said that they don't really care about him, the just want him on a leash. I said, "And you want to be more independent, don't you?" (Recognizing the metaphor.) He said, "Yup."

I then asked him to give me an example of the grinder. He said that last night he came home at midnight. They just had to know who he was with, where he had been. I said, "Sounds to me like they care about you. They worry about you, and frankly, at midnight I would worry too." Jim pouted. I waited out his silence. He said, "I don't think they care. They're just angry." I said, "Maybe they felt both—fear and anger. Do you think they had any reason to be angry last night?" He said, "Maybe so. Midnight is kind of late." I agreed. I asked him if he knew what his parents felt waiting for him. He said, "They always assume the worst. That's dumb." I said, "We all do that when we're worried." He said, "I guess I give them reasons to be angry, and I don't like it." I said, "And they don't either. I bet they feel just as bad as you do about yesterday."

I supported him in a taboo area and tried to stay close to his feelings of anger and rejection. Jim said that he was going to kill his mother one of these days. She isn't his real mom anyway. I asked him if he was angry about something she had done or angry because she isn't his real mom. (Trying to partialize his concern.) He said both. I asked him what his mom had done for him to be so upset. He said, "She is really unreal. She phoned school to insist that she'd be warned if I skipped out. It's none of her business. Dad's, sure, but not hers." I kept the issue on focus and said, "Not hers because she is your step mom?" He said, "Yup, I'm not her son. She's got no right on me." I said, "No right to care? She can't win, can she?" Jim said, "No, she can't win. She's the one who made us move from the reserve." I said I knew about that, that she wanted to make a better home for him and his dad. Jim nervously twisted his hair around his fingers and said that he would rather have the care of his mom than "her" care. I said that he had expressed real, deep feelings and that it's real hard to get over one's mom's death. (Crediting his work.)

I tried to help Jim identify the affect obstacle and offered to mediate with his parents. Jim said that he doesn't know how to tell his parents to stop calling him names when he does something wrong. Names such as *silly Indian*. When they do, his blood boils, and he goes out and gets drunk. He can't say anything. He just walks out. And he does start acting silly. I asked him to tell me what he would like exactly to tell his parents. He said that he just wants them to stop calling him names. But he can't say it to them. I said, "That's their way of criticizing you, isn't it?" He said, "Yeah. It's bad enough being told off when you do something wrong, but then calling me names like that—" "It's like you're nobody all of a sudden," I said. With tears in his eyes he replied, "Yup."

"Do you want me to help you talk to your parents?" I asked. He said, "Yeah. I can't do it alone." I suggested that I'd phone his parents and, if they agreed, we'd try to talk about the name calling and to try to understand what is behind it from their point of view. Jim said, "I don't want to talk about the things I do wrong." I replied, "You forget you do a lot of things real well, too. We have to take the bad with the good." He said, "Yeah, but I'm far from perfect." I explained that perfection is like a rainbow—nobody can reach it, we can only try. He said his parents didn't know that. I said I was sure they did, they just had high expectations for him. He said he didn't believe in high expectations. I laughed and said, "Baloney—you want to be the best about everything." He said, "How do you know?" I said that I had seen some of his carvings, that I thought they're beautiful, and that it was obvious to me that he was trying to be the best. (Emphasizing the positive). Jim had a long drawn out, "Oh." I brought the conversation back on focus and said, "So, if your parents are willing, we'll talk about both sides." He said he was willing to try but that I was going to get myself into a lot of trouble with his parents. I said, "Because I'm white?" He said, "Yeah." I said I could only try, that things should go easier if I didn't take sides. (Emphasizing the contract.)

Having broached the subject of being a white worker, the obstacle of race loses some of its power to block the working relationship. This difference will never completely disappear; however, surfacing it often makes a major difference. In the next session—the third—the worker must deal with the same issue with Jim's parents. In addition, she demonstrates her effort to understand and to work with the Native American culture by using Native metaphors.

I tried to tune in to the feelings of ambivalence of the one (Jim) and the many (the family), tried to include everyone in the communality of the experience and to clarify the contract. At the first meeting, I said that they must feel a bit uncomfortable about having a white probation officer coming into their home. Mr. Jones smiled and said, "You bet, you're the first one we managed to get in here." Mrs. Jones said that she didn't mind; she had to clean her home today for the health nurse anyway. I recognized her ambivalence and said that I know how it feels, it's a hassle to clean house because a stranger is coming in. She nodded hesitantly. I said I felt a bit like an intruder today (putting my personal feelings into words) but that I hoped we would feel more comfortable once we know each other better.

Jim's eyes were covered by his cap, and his arms crossed at his chest. I asked him what he was angry about. He said, "Nothing, leave me alone." Mrs. Jones firmly said that he couldn't talk to me like that. I said it was okay to be angry. Did they (Jim's parents) know what was making Jim so angry? (Beginning to partialize and trying to help the family members help each other.) Mr. Jones said that Jim is like that around home, not to worry. I said that maybe Jim is afraid that we might all gang up on him. (Putting client's feelings into words.) "It's certainly not my intention," I said, "I'm here to talk about a real painful issue: Jim can't stand being called a *dirty Indian,* and it hurts so much that he can't talk about it usually."

I got a nasty look from Mr. Jones. Mrs. Jones said she thought it was simple: I should forbid Jim from doing any of that crazy Indian stuff, then she'd stop calling him a crazy Indian. Mr. Jones agreed with her. I said that I know they often worry about Jim, but I can't do that. That's not my role, and it wouldn't work anyway. Jim nodded sullenly. I said that I felt uncomfortable about the phrase *crazy Indian.* (Acknowledging feelings.) I asked Jim if he knows what his parents mean by that? He lifted his cap from his eyes and said that he knew for sure "that all Indians are dirty, violent, lazy drunks." Mr. Jones said, "Here he goes again, acting crazy. Everyone knows that Indians aren't violent and drunk." Jim giggled, and Mr. Jones cracked his knuckles. I said that perhaps Jim was hitting something very painful. That was the prejudice they had to live with day in and day out. Mr. Jones said I was damn right. Mrs. Jones said that's what she worried about, that Jim would become like the rest of them Indians. I said, "You are Indian, and you aren't dirty, violent, and lazy. Neither is Jim." (Gentle demand for work.) Mrs. Jones said, "No, but that's because they'd moved away from the reserve." I said that maybe it was time to look at the positive things of the present rather than at the bad things of the past. (Emphasizing the positive and the potential to work.)

I tried to reach their feelings in their way, to establish contact, and to help the family members help each other. Jim said, "You can't help but act on impulse, that's what my breaking and entering is all about." I said, "You forget to pray to the spirit of the bear, don't you?" Mr. Jones nodded, and said I was right. He told us an Indian story about a little boy becoming a man and then a bear. It was the opposite of Jim's progress at this point, but it emphasized his potential. Jim said that the story was okay, but that the elders had better ones. I said to Jim that maybe the story hit home a bit hard. (Demand for work.) I got nowhere.

In the next section, the worker takes a risk as she tunes in on what she believes is an indirect cue about her raised by Mr. Jones, who speaks of racist "white teachers."

> Jim said that he had been kicked out of English today and that he wasn't much more disruptive than some of the white kids. I said that a little more disruption is all it takes to make a difference. Silence. Mr. Jones said that white teachers are racist. Mr. Jones said that females are more racist than men. He would fight with a white man any day, but you can't fight with a white woman. I acknowledged my feelings and said that I was afraid the arrows might start flying toward me. We all laughed, at the relief of tension. Jim said that the Indians only scalp white people who have no honor. Mr. Jones grinned. I recognize their offering and said that it felt good to hear I have honor. Their feelings for me are important to me because I respect them.
>
> I tried to put the client's feelings into words for the benefit of the other family members, so that they gain a new understanding of each other. Mrs. Jones asked me what I intended to do about Jim's alcoholism. I said Jim was doing his best to stay away from alcohol and the reserve, but sometimes he got so depressed about feeling bad about himself that he couldn't help it. Jim said it was right. He can't control himself when his parents call him a crazy Indian. Mr. Jones said that he and his wife mean well. They just don't know what else to say. I said, "I know, when you're worried, words don't come easily." Jim said gently, "When I'm rotten, why don't you just say I let you down, Dad?" Mr. Jones put his arms around his son.
>
> Mrs. Jones said that Jim was wasting his time carving, you can't make a living out of it. I said that I was really impressed by Jim's carving. They are really beautiful. Mrs. Jones said that Jim spends too much time doing that. I said that it takes a lot of time to create a piece of art. Mr. Jones said he knew, because he tried when he was younger and couldn't do half as well as Jim. Jim was beaming. He asked his dad how good an Indian dancer he was when he was younger.
>
> I offered to mediate between a system that makes it harder to communicate between Jim and his parents as a result of his delinquencies. Everyone is silent. Mrs. Jones especially looks grim. I asked if I had offended them in any way. Silence. I said, "Anything I have done or said in relation to Jim?" "No," said Mr. Jones, "I guess we are taking it out on you. Jim says that he knows what it's all about. It's about the Band." I recognized the indirect communication. "You wish you were on good terms with the Band, don't you?" Mrs. Jones said it wasn't possible. There is so much politics going on. Mr. Jones said they're arrogant. Jim continued rocking in his chair and looked hurt. I said, noting his eyes, "You feel guilty about it, you want to cry. Your breaking and entering stands in the way, doesn't it?" (Demand for work.) He nodded. I said that I would talk to the Band office. Maybe they would accept to supervise Jim's probation once I'm gone. Mr. Jones said that they refused in the past, why would they accept now? I said that they had time to get over the shock, just as Jim had time to do a lot of growing. Jim nodded. (Crediting the client's work.)

The problem has shifted in urgency. Jim and his parents are now beginning to be able to discuss the problem of Native-American identity with less anger and pain and to address other issues without approaching them from a perspective of ethnic origin. Jim's parents are beginning to be able to give him positive strokes for his ability to express his ethnic identity constructively through his beautiful carvings and his proficiency in Indian dancing, for example. Jim and his parents are striving to live together under the same roof without feeling that it is a battlefield of "good Indians" versus "bad Indians." Jim's anger has lessened, largely because he has regained the support of the elders of the band. More importantly, he has abated his delinquent behavior. The next white worker should not shy away from discussing the racial element of the interaction, because this central element permeates the life of Jim and his family. Instead, the worker should continue family work around communication patterns. For example, there are a lot of feelings of anger and sadness connected to the death of Jim's natural mother that interfere with Jim's current relationship with his stepmother. He or she should also deemphasize Jim's past record of delinquency and continue to emphasize Jim's ability and desire to do well and excel as well as his parents' desire to be the best parents. Furthermore, the worker should make an effort to enlist the elders to help provide a social support system for Jim and the family. In this example, the worker has made a start in breaking down the barriers between the parents and the child, between the family and the worker's white social service system, and between the family and the source of support in the Native community. Recognizing that a long history of communal support is central to the Native culture can be a crucial step in strengthening the family. In the child welfare study cited earlier (Shulman, 1991), regions of the provincial child welfare agency that had established effective working relationships with the Native community (e.g., friendship centers and court workers, band chiefs and elders, social workers) were found to have fewer Native children going into alternative forms of care—or if they did go into care, remaining in the Native community. Continued work with the family would require the integration of discussion on socioeconomic issues of oppression that have contributed to the struggles within the family, so that a reframing of the problem may occur from a perspective of personal pathology to that of a social perspective.

Illustrations: Students of Color With White Clients

Learning to work with culturally diverse populations can also be an important issue for students of color. In one example, an African-American student, who was placed with a Jewish family agency in the Boston area, was assigned to make a home visit to a Jewish, middle-class family who had requested help from an intake worker on coping with their teenage daughter. The first session was scheduled during a time when race relations were severely strained in the city because of a highly publicized murder case in which a white male claimed that an African-American male had shot him and murdered his pregnant wife, while they were driving home from a medical appointment. The initial public, official reaction to the case manifested the latent racism in the city. When it became apparent that the husband himself had been the murderer, the community was left with strong bitter feelings and recriminations about how quickly people were ready to accept and act on the charges.

It was within this atmosphere that the African-American student had to first tune in to her own feelings about working in the white community. Second, she had to tune in to the possible surprise of the family to finding an African–American social worker assigned to their case by a Jewish agency. In demonstrating how each student needs to develop his or her own individual artistry and strategy in his or her work, the student addressed the issue right from the start. When the door opened, the father greeted her with a subtle, but discernable look of surprise. She responded, "Not quite what you expected," and then laughed, as did he. After settling into the living room, she said: "I don't think you expected an African-American worker to visit with you, and if it is an issue for you, we can discuss it." He admitted that he had been surprised but that he was more interested in whether she could help his family than in her race. The contracting session moved well after this opening and ongoing work was established with the family. The student had decided to deal with the issue head on in her own unique way; others might have waited until the issue was perceived to be a problem. Either way, there is a good chance that unless openly identified at some point in the work, race might remain an issue under the surface, thus creating an illusion of work.

It is important to recognize that such issues are not always dealt with and dismissed forever—even when addressed directly. They may reemerge at points in the relationship, needing further discussion. The student, in this example, reported on an individual session with the father late in the middle phase of work, after they had established a positive, warm working relationship, in which they had shared a laugh with each other over an incident. The student reached out to poke the father in the arm in a spontaneous response to his story and then stopped half way. The client said: "You wouldn't have stopped if I were black." After a moment of reflection, the student agreed and then wondered if they should discuss the race issue again to see if perhaps it was having an impact on their work. In the resulting discussion, the father revealed how helpful the student had been to him and his family and that he was beginning to realize they would be missing her after termination.

In another example, an Asian–American social worker had to deal with another common issue faced by members of any minority group when a client reveals offensive attitudes or beliefs. In this example, she was working with an elder service agency assigned to an elderly, Italian-American woman living alone in a housing project. Recent changes in the demographics of the neighborhood had resulted in the departure of Italian-American residents, many of whom had been friends of this client, and their replacement by Asian-American immigrants.

During the first visit, the client, apparently completely ignoring the race of the worker, described with anger her feelings about all of the Chinese in the building. The client complained about their sitting together outside of the building, their use of the Chinese language and their "strange" ways. The worker was shocked at the anger and racism expressed toward the Asian-American residents but felt blocked in her ability to respond. She was angry and was afraid of what she might say.

After presenting the example at a workshop she was better able to tune in to her own feelings toward the racist comments as well as the underlying feelings of the client who had experienced many losses. It became clearer to the worker that the way the client related to her (the process) was directly related to the content. At her next session with the client, she said: "I have to let you know that as an Asian American I myself have experienced as very painful what you have said about your neighbors. People from my culture are very different and you seem not to understand much about them. I realize you are also very hurt under all of your anger since you have lost most of your friends from the building and must feel very alone." This response, both the sharing of appropriate professional feelings and the exploration of the client's pain under the anger, demonstrates a good integration of professional and personal at what must be a difficult time for the worker. It also led to the client apologizing to the worker and then starting to cry as the losses were described.

Supervision approaches. It is crucial for the supervisor to model the dynamics and skills involved in working with diverse populations by addressing these taboo issues in the field instructor-student relationship. It could be very difficult, for example, for a student of color to discuss issues related to clients of color with a white field instructor. The instructor would have to be sensitive to the possible barriers and be ready to respond directly to indirect cues if they emerge.

This is illustrated in an excerpt from an early interview between a white supervisor and a Native student who was a mature woman but new to training. The student described, with much feeling, a court case that she had sat in on in which, she felt, a white lawyer had made racist remarks while supposedly defending a Native mother who wanted her child returned. The lawyer had asked a witness if she had ever heard of "Native time," implying that it was common for Natives to be late. The student described how she had confronted the lawyer during a recess and told him how she felt about the comment. After some discussion about her anger at the insensitivity of certain white professionals, the supervisor approached the authority theme this way:

SUPERVISOR: Can I just stop for a minute? I'm just wondering, just going back to what you were saying about what we should be sensitive to. You're talking about white professionals—well, I'm a white social worker, so I'm wondering maybe I should also be addressing that. I'm also wondering how that applies to me. How can you help me be sensitive to yourself and your Native culture so that I can be helpful to you in this situation and also grow myself? I have to be helpful to you in this, and obviously, you're Native and I'm white. You have something to teach me in this. Let's do a tuning in exercise for me.

STUDENT: I think perhaps you could address that. These issues aren't raised for me until I see a Native client in such a situation. I would be more apt to stick up for myself. I don't think you have to be as conscious of race in dealing with me.

SUPERVISOR: I'm not sure that I'm saying that. I'm just saying, help me tune in to what I should be aware of—not necessarily in you—but in the clients I deal with, or in the people that I supervise, who by and large are going to be white. I'm probably not going to be supervising that many Native social workers, because, unfortunately, there's not that many of you around. What should I be aware of? I think I see racism when it's there. I pick it up, obviously. But how can I be sensitive to . . . .

STUDENT: I have an excellent book that you might like to look at. I'll bring it in next Wednesday. But, I think, more than that—realize that a Native, especially an older one . . . say, from age 30 on, is not apt to disagree with you, even if you're respecting their rights.

SUPERVISOR: Would you disagree with me?

STUDENT: Yeah, I would. But, very likely, it would be like when that client came up and talked to the family support worker in court, and said, "I don't want you to worry about . . . feeling bad about testifying against me." The social worker said, "Now isn't that terrific! I mean, she's a real trooper. She knows that the truth is the truth." Actually, in my view, that client was saying: "Please don't be mad at me; and don't think I'm mad at you and react badly to me." I'm making an awful lot of assumptions, and perhaps I'm completely off base.

SUPERVISOR: You're making your assumptions from your perspective, from your cultural and personal perspective. And maybe they're right. Most likely, they're right.

STUDENT: My idea is that she wouldn't have had the self-confidence to go up and say: "Look, you bitch, I let you in my home every day and . . . ."

SUPERVISOR: I'm asking you to be sensitive to your assumptions. Let's say you were the client's social worker. You're a Native social worker dealing with a client. Being sensitive to your assumptions and to the cultural similarities that you have, how is that going to affect the way you work with her?

STUDENT: I would not take her first answer as being her true feelings.

SUPERVISOR: Okay.

STUDENT: Like, if I said, "How do you feel about me coming in every morning?" and the client said, "That's really nice of you to do something for me." I would look at that as the client trying to be nice to *me*.

SUPERVISOR: Would that be any different for a white client?

STUDENT: I think I would look at it that way if it was anybody that I felt was feeling in a one-down position, like badly in a one-down position.

SUPERVISOR: I think that I would ask you to be sensitive to the fact that it's a function of maybe being *Native*, if there's such a word, but it's also a function of being one-down anyway. And if you were dealing with a white client, by and large that white client would say back to you, "Oh, I'm feeling fine about you being here," when actually they want to say, "You bitch, get out of my house." I think it's really important for you to remember, the client is one-down, more than the client is Native. The client may feel two-down if they're also Native. They still have to deal with an authority thing going on there, whether the authority is Native or white or whether the client is Native or white. I think part of your learning is to really be aware that the client is one-down anyway and that by and large a white client would say the same thing back.

STUDENT: That is quite possible, but I think Natives might be better at hiding their true feelings.

SUPERVISOR: Right! And that's probably where your sensitivity to what's going on under there is really good.

Although the worker did not take up the supervisor's offer to explore this area further, perhaps feeling hesitant in a first session, the supervisor did make it clear that this could be an agenda item. The supervisor might also have dropped it, feeling it was too threatening to the worker in a first interview. However, she did point to the issue of authority in terms of the worker's relationship with clients, as a Native working with Native or white clients. Thus, this sensitive subject was brought out in the open for future work. Again, this excerpt is an example of the parallel between supervision and practice. The discussion goes from the supervisor's concern with the student to the student's concern with clients.

MONITORING AND EVALUATING STUDENT SKILL DEVELOPMENT

Supervisors are most directly involved in monitoring the skill development of beginning students; however, some ongoing supervision must also be provided for advanced students. The process of examining skill development contributes to effective practice at any level.[5]

Supervision of First-Year or Beginning Students

This section discusses the order and timing of skill development for beginning students, to give supervisors a general standard against which students' progress can be measured and evaluated. The discussion applies to students' professional development during the first six months of field practice. It assumes they have had a varied case load, a chance to discuss the work with a supervisor, and other training opportunities. (Appendix B provides guidelines.)

The following pattern can be expected in developing practice skills: At the end of six months, students should have some basic skill in clearly defining statements of their purpose and role, and they should be making efforts to reach for client feedback. In initial interviews, students should be tuned in to the client's feelings and concerns; and in the first sessions, they should be prepared to address the issue of the authority theme as it emerges. It is probable that they will have difficulty with strong negative feelings from clients: Precisely, students will need more experience to develop the confidence to handle difficult clients and to make demands for work in the face of strong client resistance.

At this stage, students should be listening for indirect cues, although they may find them hard to pick up in the initial sessions. In the first months, students should be able to show their interest and concern for clients. They should be listening and trying to understand the client's problems and point of view as well as learning to contain themselves until they are clear about the sessional contract. Moreover, their effort in dealing with feelings will be apparent in tentative steps to reach for the client's affect and to articulate the feelings. Efforts to deal with affect will often seem artificial as students struggle to develop ways of putting feelings into their own words. These skills should be strengthened during the first year. Imitation of the supervisor may be a first step in this process.

The skill of reaching for negative feedback will not be evident until students develop greater confidence in the work. This often comes after the first year. The ability to share feelings spontaneously is a difficult skill to develop, but there should be evidence that it is being used with greater freedom during the second year. The

---

[5] For guidelines on student field performance, see Appendix B.

skill of sharing data *when relevant* should also be evidenced, as well as a willingness to leave the client free to accept the student's ideas, or not.

As this summary suggests, there should be limited expectations for skill development by beginning students. Actual progress will vary, depending on what students bring to the situation and the success of the supervisory relationship. The supervisor must not forget how difficult the development of core skills can be or be too easily frustrated by the time required for students to develop these skills. If contracting, listening, empathy, and evidence of honest expression of feelings emerge in the first six months, students should be considered to be learning the skills satisfactorily.

Supervision of Second-Year or Experienced Students

With experienced students, the supervisor must be sensitive to the possible defensiveness caused by guilt feelings about past cases. Being asked to discuss a particular piece of work with a supervisor often recalls associations to other clients. In such a session, student's eyes may take on a dazed expression as they appear to turn off. The supervisor who recognizes that students may be associating to past clients has an opportunity to explore student's feelings about unsatisfactory client experiences. Experienced students who appear defensive on a particular issue are often sending a signal to the supervisor that the area is one in which they have self-doubts. At this point, students need a great deal of support to help them moderate their harsh views of themselves. The supervisor should point out that students have only been able to offer clients what they had at the time they worked with them, and they should not hold themselves responsible for more than that. They need to focus, instead, on what they will do for their present and future clients. Helping students to be less harsh on themselves and less judgmental on others is often the most important way a supervisor can help them open up their practice to a continuous process of learning from their experiences.

Supervisors are most directly involved in monitoring the skill development of beginning students; however, some ongoing supervision must also be provided for those with experience. Thus, the process of examining skill development contributes to effective practice at any level of the student's experience.

RESEARCH FINDINGS

This section summarizes a number of findings related to supervision content, context, and process. Some of these findings are drawn from two supervision studies undertaken by the author (Shulman, 1981; Shulman, 1991; Shulman, Robinson & Luckyj, 1981) as well as from the literature.[6]

Content and Context of Supervision

In the first supervision study conducted in 1981 (Shulman and Shulman et al.), workers in the field were asked to identify what they would like to have discussed in their supervision contacts, as compared with the actual contact content. Their first preference was that supervisors should devote more time to teaching practice skills, followed by more time on discussing research information and on providing feedback on performance. Such supervision-consulting roles also were the favored tasks of supervisors queried in the study.

Other findings in respect to the content of supervision, contact frequency, and the educational role of the supervisor included the following. Positive correlations were found between a supervisor's helpfulness and the percentage of time invested in the teaching role ($r = .32$), the sharing of research findings and child welfare theory ($r = .50$), the worker's perception of the supervisor as being knowledgeable about policies and procedures ($r = .61$), and a supervisor's sharing of data ($r = .65$).

Other research has supported the idea that both supervisors and supervisees regard the educational function of supervision as important and a source of satisfaction. In the Kadushin (1973) study, two of the three strongest sources of supervisor satisfaction were found to be related to helping the supervisee to grow and develop professionally and to sharing social work knowledge and skill. In the same study, *workers* indicated that two of the three main sources of their satisfaction with supervision were receiving help in dealing with clients and in developing as professionals. In another study by Scott (1969), workers expressed a preference for supervisors who knew their theoretical fundamentals, were skilled in teaching, and were capable of offering professional assistance.

Heppner and Roehlke (1984) examined supervision in the related field of counseling psychology, using data from surveys of counselors in training. Their findings were similar to those of the studies just cited. Supervisor roles, which included

---

[6] For full discussions of this research, see the cited reports as well as three of this author's recent publications: *Interactional Supervision*, Washington, DC: National Association of Social Workers, 1993; *The Skills of Helping Individuals, Families and Groups* (3rd ed.), Itasca, IL: F. E. Peacock, 1992; and *Interactional Social Work Practice: Toward an Empirical Theory*, Itasca, IL: F. E. Peacock, 1991.

behaviors that helped trainees to assess their strengths and increase their self-confidence, were positively associated with trainee's perceptions of their supervisors competence, trainee's satisfaction with supervision, and trainee's perception of the supervisor's contribution to their increased counseling ability.

In a 1979 study of 16 supervisors and 31 practicum students in counseling psychology, Worthington and Roehlke examined the association between 42 supervisory behaviors and the perceptions of effective supervisory behavior on the part of the supervisors. They found that supervisors generally perceived their ability to provide good supervision as offering feedback to the students. Beginning students, however, rated supervision as good if a personal, pleasant supervisory-supervisee relationship existed; the supervisor structured conferences, especially during the early sessions; and the supervisor taught how to counsel (by example and through the literature and didactic presentation) and then encouraged the student to try out the skills.

Similar findings were also observed by Pincus (1986). In a questionnaire survey of 327 hospital nurses, a positive communications climate between supervisor and worker and feedback on skills were associated with job satisfaction and job performance. In a study by Gondolfo and Brown (1987), when 102 clinical psychology interns rated the supervision they were receiving and determined what ideal supervision would be, the interns reported viewing a positive supervisor as being in a collaborative role and functioning as a facilitator who promoted problem solving. They also indicated they wanted to observe more of their supervisors' clinical work, to have their supervisors observe their work, and to experience a more open process of evaluative feedback. Ideal supervisors were seen as warm, interactive, and direct with feedback.

For another type of analysis, in the 1981 study (Shulman et al.), a number of scales were created, consisting of the average score on two or more variables for each supervisor. The supervisors were then ranked in order of their scores on these scales, and for each scale, the top 25% (approximately) and the bottom 25% were identified. (These are described on the following page.) These two contrasting groups were then compared on the scores they received from their workers on another scale that combined relationship ("In general, how satisfied are you with your working relationship with your supervisor?") and helpfulness ("In general, how helpful is your supervisor?").

One of the scales was an index of supervisors' satisfaction with their role. The percentage of time they reported they would like to invest in each task was simply subtracted from the percentage they indicated they *actually* did invest. The absolute differences (disregarding positive or negative signs) for each task were summed to produce the index of role satisfaction. When the group of 18 supervisors who were highly satisfied with their role was compared with the group of 21 who indicated low satisfaction, there was no difference in workers' responses on the relationship-helpfulness scale. Thus, supervisors' satisfaction with their roles did not seem to affect how their workers judged their working relationship and their helpfulness.

The findings were different when worker satisfaction with supervision content was examined. Employing a similar procedure, the absolute differences between the actual content of supervision and preferred content were summed, and an index of worker content satisfaction was computed. Then, the supervisors were ordered from those with the least satisfied workers to those with the most satisfied. When the 25 supervisors with the most satisfied workers were compared with the 28 with the least satisfied, a significant difference was found on the relationship-helpfulness scale in favor of the supervisors with more satisfied workers ($p = .02$).

Thus, the data appeared to support the argument that workers' satisfaction with the content of supervision was a factor in how they judged their supervisors, and supervisors' role satisfaction did not seem to have any impact. Because the theoretical model guiding the study assumed that factors associated with the content, context, and process of supervision would be important contributors to supervision effectiveness, these findings offer some support for the model.

The question of supervisor availability was an important one in this analysis, correlating with a great number of other variables. For example, availability correlated positively with the working relationship (.40), the ability of the worker to talk openly with the supervisor (.41), the provision of a supportive atmosphere (.35), and the supervisor's helpfulness (.47). In addition, supervisors who were available were also seen as demonstrating an ability to clarify the role of the supervisor ($r = .26$); help the worker discuss taboo subjects (.31); understand the worker's feelings (.39); articulate the worker's feelings (.25); partialize the worker's concerns (.28); and provide relevant data (.33).

In considering the meaning of these correlations, the problem of not being able to determine the direction of influence must be recognized. Are supervisors who are available able to demonstrate their capacity for empathy, for example, whereas those who are not available cannot do so? Or do supervisors who are more empathic make themselves more available? The author's own experience suggests that both statements are partially true. These findings raise a question as to how workers actually interpreted the phrase *available when I need him or her*. Although the question was meant to get at supervisors' allocation of time, for some workers, it may have meant being emotionally available when needed.

Whatever the inferences—and different ones are possible and very reasonable— the findings suggest that the context of supervision does have some impact on supervisor effectiveness (although it may not be simply a question of how much regularly scheduled time is provided). While regularly scheduled individual and group time appears to be important, no specific pattern is identified as the right one. Conceivably, although a supervisor may hold regularly scheduled individual conferences with a worker, because of the worker's lack of satisfaction with content or the supervisor's lack of skill, the worker might still say: "My supervisor was not there when I needed him or her." Another supervisor might meet on a less regular schedule and, yet, always be available when needed.

The method of comparing groups of supervisors on context factors added supporting evidence to these inferences. For example, a scale on contact regularity was computed by combining a worker's responses to the questions on the regularity of individual and group sessions. The 26 supervisors with the lowest scores on regularity were compared with the 26 supervisors with the highest scores. There was a significant difference in their scores on the relationship-helpfulness scale, favoring supervisors with the higher levels of regularity ($p = .000$). A second scale on supervisor availability was constructed by combining the contact regularity items with the question, Was the supervisor available when needed? This scale also produced significant differences between the 26 supervisors with the lowest scores and the 26 with the highest, also favoring those who were considered the most available ($p = .000$).

In the author's more recent study (Shulman, 1991), analysis of similar variables supported these general findings on the importance of contextual variables such as frequency of meetings and the availability of the supervisor when needed. These were found across all three levels of agency management (executive-manager, manager-supervisor, and supervisor-worker). One difference indicated that the lower the level of the supervision pair, the greater the supervisor's availability when needed.

The Impact of Supervisory Skill

A number of the skills described in this monograph were incorporated into the worker questionnaire in earlier study of supervision skill (Shulman et al., 1981) and then reexamined in the 1992 (Shulman) study. These skills include putting the worker's feelings into words, supporting the worker in taboo areas, understanding the worker's feelings, sharing thoughts and feelings, partializing the worker's concerns, dealing with the theme of authority, providing data, and demonstrating a knowledge of policy and procedures. A number of findings are summarized in this section.

In the first stages of supervision, the ability of the supervisor to view a case from the perspective of the worker and to develop a preliminary empathy with them is an important skill. By developing this sensitivity to the worker's indirect cues, the supervisor is better able to respond directly to the worker. In earlier studies, there was no way to determine the supervisor's use of the tuning-in skill, but it was possible to measure a skill that should be enhanced by tuning in: the skill of putting the worker's feelings into words. The item on the questionnaire designed to measure this skill was worded as follows: "My supervisor can sense my feelings without my having to put them into words." In the 1991 study, the worker could select a response from among the following five options: (1) strongly agree, (2) agree, (3) uncertain, (4) disagree, and (5) strongly disagree. The same response categories were employed to measure most of the skill items.

A number of workers in the 1981 study (Shulman et al.) underlined the importance of this skill with comments such as, "It is important for both client and worker that the qualities of empathy are found in a supervisor." Other workers commented on their supervisors' lack of being tuned in, for example: "Many times I have the feeling that my supervisor is not really interested in what I have to say—is preoccupied."

In the 1991 study (Shulman), 40% of managers agreed or strongly agreed that their executives were able to put their feelings into words, although only 21% of supervisors agreed (although none strongly) that their managers demonstrated that same skill. As for workers, only 4% strongly agreed, and 22.5% agreed that supervisors articulated their feelings for them. All three levels of adminstration scored lower on the use of this skill than their workers did when rated by their clients. This may be a reflection of a confusion over the appropriate place of the empathic skills in supervision and the concern over not "doing therapy" with staff.

When correlations between the use of this skill by frontline supervisors and supervisory outcomes were examined in the 1991 study (Shulman), a pattern of significant positive associations emerged. These included positive correlations with the social worker's perception of rapport with the supervisor (.79) and trust (.75). In addition, a positive association with the social worker's morale (.49) and perception of availability of peer group support (.44) was noted. The strong association between the use of this skill and rapport and trust was also found when the manager-supervisor level of interaction was examined.

In the 1982 study, the item measuring the skill of exploring taboo subjects appeared on the worker questionnaire as follows: "My supervisor helps me to talk about subjects that are not comfortable to discuss (e.g., my reactions to working with clients around sexual issues)." On average, the workers gave supervisors in the study a score of 3, that is, "sometimes." The skill was positively correlated with supervisor helpfulness (r = .70).

These findings parallel those in the author's past research on social work practice (Shulman, 1978, 1981, 1991, 1992). For a worker to feel free enough to discuss uncomfortable areas, a good relationship with the supervisor is crucial. Because many of the most difficult aspects of practice are associated with taboo areas (e.g., sex, death, money) and because help cannot be offered if the areas are not directly discussed, this is a crucial supervision skill.

The skill of understanding workers' feelings was phrased on the questionnaire as follows: "When I tell my supervisor how I feel, she or he understands (e.g., my own frustrations with a client)." The average supervisor score indicated that supervisors were able to understand "a good part of the time." The positive correlation (r = .70) of this skill with helpfulness was also one of the stronger findings. This is similar to the importance attached to this skill in a number of areas of research on the helping professions, including social work, psychoanalysis, nursing, medicine, and teaching.

In supervision research, Kadushin (1973) found that receiving emotional support was described by 21% of the workers surveyed as the strongest source of satisfaction with their supervision. Another study by Olmstead and Christenson (1973) used a standardized, leadership opinion questionnaire to study 228 social work supervisors in three settings. Scales used in this study made it possible to rate supervisors in social work on consideration (mutual trust, respect for ideas, consideration of feelings, and warmth in the relationship). These supervisors could then be compared with supervisors in other fields. Social work supervisors were among the highest rated supervisors on the consideration scale, and providing support was described as what social work supervisors did best. Another finding of the Olmstead and Christenson study was that satisfaction with supervision itself is positively associated with satisfaction with the agency, positive individual performance, less absenteeism, agency competence, and agency performance.

On the issue of keeping the supervisory function clear in relation to discussion of personnel problems, in Kadushin's study, workers indicated that supervisors were not too involved in dealing with their personal problems. Supervisors, more often than workers, viewed the legitimate source of help for job-related personal problems as outside of the supervisory relationship. Presented with the statement whether they would want the supervisor to help them if personal problems came up in their work with clients, 48% of workers agreed compared with only 30% of supervisors.

The skill of sharing thoughts and feelings was worded on the questionnaire as follows: "My supervisor shares his or her thoughts and feelings (e.g., sharing frustrations around a work situation)." The average score indicated that supervisors were able to do this between "sometimes" and "a good part of the time." The positive correlation with helpfulness was lower on this item (r = .53) than on most of the other supervisory skills examined.

The skill of partializing the worker's concerns was worded on the questionnaire as follows: "My supervisor helps me sort out my concerns in a situation and look at them one at a time." Supervisors were rated as demonstrating this skill between "sometimes" and "a good part of the time." Its positive correlation with helpfulness was one of the highest of the study (r = .77).

The item on the worker's questionnaire dealing with the use of authority attempted to measure the supervisor's efforts to encourage feedback, particularly negative feedback, on the part of the worker. It was worded as follows: "When I am upset about something my supervisor says or does, he/she encourages me to talk about it." The supervisors in this study also fared well on this item, with an average score halfway between "sometimes" and "a good part of the time." The positive correlation for this skill with helpfulness was also quite high ($r = .75$).

Workers in this study made most of their comments in respect to the issue of authority. Some examples were:

- My supervisor has a strong authoritarian role.
- My supervisor should feel secure enough in his or her self not to feel threatened by a question or a suggestion.
- My supervisor has a good sense of fair play.
- My supervisor has an excellent capacity to give workers independence, yet to keep track of what they are doing.
- I especially appreciate the flexibility with which my supervisor deals with different employees' needs and his or her responsiveness to personal work styles.
- My present supervisor is the best I've ever had—what has impressed me the most is the willingness to look at his or her own shortcomings and to work on them.

Other research on the issue of authority has suggested that it plays an important part in the supervision process. For example, Mayer and Rosenblatt (1975) found that workers who felt secure with supervisors also felt less anxious with their clients. In the Olmstead and Christenson study, when social work supervisors were rated on a scale measuring structure (exercise of control and authority), they were found to be the lowest in exercise of authority of the 36 professional groups examined. This conforms to Kadushin's finding that the exercise of authority is one reason for supervisors' strong dissatisfaction with the job. These findings offer evidence in support of the idea that the integration of support and demand is difficult for human service supervisors.

The 1981 study (Shulman et al.) attempted to get at the issue of providing data through two items. In the first, they asked workers to assess their supervisors' knowledge of policy and procedure with the following item: "My supervisor has a detailed and accurate grasp of policy and procedures." In the second, they asked if the supervisor shared their views by presenting the statement: "My supervisor shares his or her suggestions about the subjects we discuss for my consideration." On the first question, supervisors in the study received very positive scores and were rated as being knowledgeable between "a good part of the time" and "most or all of the time." The positive correlation of this item with helpfulness was $r = .61$. As for the second item, supervisors shared their views "a good part of the time," and the correlation of this item with helpfulness was $r = .65$.

These findings were as expected. In Kadushin's study, both supervisors and workers rated "expert power" as the main source of influence of a supervisor. In the Olmstead and Christenson study, "expert power" was the first source of influence when ranked by workers, with "positional power" second, "referent (relationship) power" third, and "reward and coercive power" last.

Workers' comments in the author's study dealt with the supervisor's knowledge and the sharing of information. Some examples of comments were:

- My supervisor has difficulty making decisions regarding a particular case. He or she has never carried a case load and thus is not knowledgeable.

- My supervisor should ask what a worker feels he or she wants to do with a case before giving his or her suggestion of what he or she would do.

The skill of encouraging the worker to raise concerns, which is crucial for the development of trust in the supervisor-worker relationship, was phrased on the worker's questionnaire as follows: "I can talk openly to my supervisor about job-related concerns." The 5-point scale ranging from "none of the time" to "most or all of the time" was used. The average score was positive on this item, with workers reporting they could talk openly slightly better than "a good part of the time." One positive characteristic described was that of the supervisor as "open and straight-forward and very approachable." In contrast, some supervisors were described as "very critical and hard to approach," or simply "too defensive."

The supervisor's ability to develop a supportive atmosphere has also been found to be significant. This factor was borrowed from the Kadushin study and was worded on the worker's questionnaire as follows: "My supervisor creates the kind of emotional atmosphere in which I feel free to discuss my mistakes and failures as well as my successes." On average, supervisors in the study were rated positively on this factor, with a rating close to "a good part of the time." The following comments give a flavor of the reactions of those workers who thought they had a supportive supervisor, as well as those who felt they did not:

- He or she backs me up!
- I get moral support in times of stress.
- My supervisor works with me, providing the help and information as I ask—gives me a real feeling of accomplishment.
- My supervisor has a genuine concern for his workers' well-being.
- I feel free to share my inadequacies and to ask for help when I need it.
- My supervisor's emotional support and praise of my efforts is really what keeps me going.
- Workers really need to feel appreciated by their supervisors.
- My supervisor is inclined to favor one worker and spend more time with that person than the rest of the staff.
- I would like my supervisor to discuss my mistakes and failures more frequently than once a year at evaluation.
- There is a lack of support in all areas from my supervisor and upper management.

Finally, dealing with authority issues in the supervisor-client relationship is important to the success of supervision. Particularly difficult is working out an understanding of workers' limits of authority, their ability to take responsibility, and so on, in a way which allows workers some freedom, while still recognizing the supervisor's accountability. Using another item borrowed from the Kadushin questionnaire, workers were asked to comment on the following: "My supervisor permits me to make my own mistakes (in those areas in which I have discretion within the boundaries of policies and procedures)." In the author's study, the average supervisor was rated as being able to do this "a good part of the time."

The Parallel Process in Supervision

The concept of the parallel processes in work with clients and supervision of staff is based on the similarity of the dynamics of supervision and worker-client dynamics. Doehrman's (1972) study of 8 sets of concurrent supervisor-supervisee relationships over a 20-week period indicated that behavioral patterns in the supervisor-worker interaction are similar to those in the worker-client engagement. A study by Arlow (1963) also supported this position.

This concept also suggests that supervisors themselves need help and support if they are to provide these for their students. The author's own supervision study found that access to ongoing emotional support was associated with being an effective supervisor.

Impact of the Supervisor's Job Stress and Manageability

Most field instructors take on the task of supervising a practicum student as an additional responsibility with limited, if any, relief from their overall job responsibilities. Under normal conditions, instructors are able to integrate the additional time needed into their normal work load. With increased stress resulting from more complex and demanding caseloads, as well as the stress resulting from cutbacks and cost-containment efforts, even the best-intentioned field instructor finds him or herself under great pressure. The following findings related to stress and job manageability have relevance to today's reality in the human services field.

Positive significant associations between lower supervisor stress and availability to the social workers (.19), implementation of the consulting role (.36), capacity to empathize with workers (.22), and the workers' ability to talk openly to their supervisors (.18), all supported the hypotheses that lower stress for the supervisor is associated with the supervisor's effectiveness (Shulman, 1991).

Other studies have also pointed to stress and job manageability as important factors. In one study of supervisors' work loads in a public welfare agency, Galm (1972) found that supervisors simply did not have enough time to supervise. In the Kadushin study of 469 supervisors, 53% ($n = 249$) indicated that not having time to supervise was one of the strongest sources of their dissatisfaction with the job. For 27% ($n = 127$), having to make decisions without clear guidelines was a strong source of dissatisfaction.

In spite of the data on job stress and job manageability difficulties, some supervisors may use these factors to explain supervisors' lack of activity in certain areas of supervision when other factors, such as lack of confidence or skills, are also hampering them. When the author pressed supervisors in workshops, many admitted they could provide more help, even within the limitations of the job. This experience led him to assume that stress and manageability, by themselves, would not be crucial factors affecting supervision effectiveness for most supervisors. For some supervisors, they might be the only factors, but on the whole, other factors might be more crucial. Some stressed supervisors holding jobs they often found unmanageable could nevertheless provide significant help to their workers, while other unstressed supervisors holding manageable jobs might provide limited help.

Summary

The dynamics and skills of the educational function of supervision discussed in this chapter are based on underlying assumptions about teaching and learning. Supervisors' knowledge of the subject area and ability to transmit ideas clearly are central to teaching, but they are only part of the process. The task for supervisors is to *mediate between the learner and the subject areas to be learned*. In teaching core practice skills, supervisors must demonstrate the same skills they teach. Modeling the use of these skills in supervision practice is an effective way of teaching their use in the student-client context.

A basis for monitoring and evaluating the development of these skills can be found in a profile of the skill development pattern exhibited by the average new student. The suggestions provided for dealing with the special problems of educational supervision of experienced students can become a standard for evaluating their progress.

Appendix A

Sample Written Exercises for Client Assessment and Student Self-Evaluation

This section provides sample, written self-evaluation exercises that students can use to systematically evaluate their own work. Intended to be introduced during supervision conferences throughout the year, these ungraded, self-evaluation exercises are designed to help the student and field instructor strengthen their assessment and practice skills.

Client Socioeconomic Context Inventory

This assignment has three parts. Part I is designed to develop your ability to assess a client's socioeconomic stress level. Part II asks you to develop an analysis of the potential impact of these stressors on a client's vulnerability and his or her ability to use help. Part III asks you to develop an intervention plan designed to increase the client's ability to use help.

Part I - Client Assessment

Select a client, either an individual or a family or group member. Rate this client on each item on the 5-point agreement scale as follows: (1) strongly agree, (2) agree, (3) uncertain, (4) disagree, or (5) strongly disagree. Provide a brief explanation supporting your rating (e.g., systematic gender discrimination or exploitation, poor self-image resulting from oppression related to race, ethnicity, or socioeconomic status, or job discrimination related to sexual orientation).

RATING:

In my opinion, this client is, or has been, affected by oppression related to his or her . . .

		Strongly Agree	Agree	Uncertain	Disagree	Strongly Disagree
		1	2	3	4	5
a.	gender	☐	☐	☐	☐	☐
b.	race or ethnicity	☐	☐	☐	☐	☐
c.	sexual orientation	☐	☐	☐	☐	☐
d.	mental health	☐	☐	☐	☐	☐
e.	physical or mental impairment	☐	☐	☐	☐	☐
f.	socioeconomic class	☐	☐	☐	☐	☐
g.	other (please explain).	☐	☐	☐	☐	☐

EXPLANATION: _____

_____

_____

_____

Part II - Analysis of the Assessment

_____

_____

_____

_____

_____

Part III - Intervention Plan to Increase Client Ability to Use Help

_____

_____

_____

_____

_____

Client Stress, Acceptance, Motivation, Ability, and Support Inventory

This assignment has three parts. Part I is designed to develop your ability to assess a client's problem, as well as his or her stress level, acceptance of the problem, level of motivation, ability to use help, and social support system. Part II asks you to develop an analysis of the interaction of these five elements. Part III asks you to develop an intervention plan that is designed to increase the client's ability to use help.

Part I - Client Assessment
Select a client, either an individual or a family or group member. Rate this client on each item below, using a 5-point agreement scale as follows: (1) strongly agree, (2) agree, (3) uncertain, (4) disagree, or (5) strongly disagree. Provide a brief explanation supporting your rating (e.g., patterns of behavior or client comments that either indicate strong or weak motivation or process excerpts that demonstrate denial of the problem).

RATING:
In my opinion, this client . . .

	Strongly Agree	Agree	Uncertain	Disagree	Strongly Disagree
	1	2	3	4	5
a. is in agreement that there is a problem.	☐	☐	☐	☐	☐
b. has found their problem very stressful.	☐	☐	☐	☐	☐
c. is highly motivated to work on the problem presently.	☐	☐	☐	☐	☐
d. is capable of dealing with the problem with the help provided.	☐	☐	☐	☐	☐
e. has adequate practical support available.	☐	☐	☐	☐	☐
f. has adequate emotional support available.	☐	☐	☐	☐	☐

EXPLANATION: _____

_____

_____

_____

Part II - Analysis of the Interaction of Part I Variables

_____

_____

_____

_____

_____

Part III - Intervention Plan to Increase the Client's Ability to Use Help

_____

_____

_____

_____

_____

Student Self-Assessment Skill

The following exercise is designed to help you to assess your skill use in your work with clients. Part I asks you to rate yourself in comparison to the average scores for workers reported in the author's study of social work practice skill. Part II asks you to identify barriers that make the use of particular skills difficult for you. Part III asks you to identify strategies for strengthening your use of these skills.

Part I - Skill Assessment

The following set of eight skills were identified in the Shulman study (1991) as important for developing an effective working relationship. The first column next to each skill reports the average score reported for workers in the cited study. The scale is as follows: (1) never, (2) rarely, (3) fairly often, and (4) often. Enter your self-assessment about your own mastery of the skill. Take into account an average score, based on your practice with all clients.

HELPING CLIENTS TO MANAGE THEIR FEELINGS

	Average Score	Student
Reaching Inside of Silences	2.35	
Articulating Client's Feelings	2.65	
Displaying Understanding of Client's Feelings	3.02	
Sharing Worker's Feelings	2.14	

HELPING CLIENTS TO MANAGE THEIR PROBLEMS

	Average Score	Student
Clarifying Worker's Purpose and Role	3.08	
Reaching for Client Feedback	2.62	
Partializing Client Concerns	2.65	
Supporting Clients in Taboo Areas	2.45	

Part II - Barriers to Skill Use

The many types of barriers to skill use include professional inexperience, lack of knowledge, limited life experience, particularly difficult clients or problems (e.g., sexual abuse), and so forth. Use the following lines to identify your barriers in relation to those skills on which you rated yourself lower than average or those that you would like to use more often in your practice.

1. _____

2. _____

3. _____

4. _____

5. _____

6. _____

Part III - Strategies for Strengthening Skill Use
Identify specific steps you will take to attempt to overcome barriers to skill use (e.g., tuning in to a particular client, role playing with your field instructor, initiating a discussion with colleagues about particularly difficult clients or taboo issues).

1. _____

2. _____

3. _____

4. _____

5. _____

6. _____

Student Self-Analysis of Client Working Relationship

The following exercise is designed to help you to assess your working relationship and helpfulness with a specific client. You are asked to put yourself in your client's shoes and attempt to assess how your client would respond if asked these questions. Part I asks you to rate the elements of the relationship. Part II asks you to identify barriers for both the worker and the client that make it difficult to strengthen the relationship. Part III asks you to identify strategies for attempting to overcome these barriers.

Part I - Relationship Assessment

		Never	Rarely	Fairly Often	Often
		1	2	3	4
a.	Does this client feel he or she can talk openly to you about anything on his or her mind?	☐	☐	☐	☐
b.	Does this client feel comfortable in discussing with you her or his mistakes and failures, as well as successes?	☐	☐	☐	☐
c.	Does this client feel that you are interested in and concerned about them as clients in their own right?	☐	☐	☐	☐

		Another Agenda	Mostly Another Agenda	Mostly Helping	Just Helping
		1	2	3	4
d.	Does this client feel you are there to help with his or her concerns, as he or she perceives them, or that you have another agenda (e.g., trying to change them or investigate them)?	☐	☐	☐	☐

		Not At All Helpful	Not Very Helpful	Helpful	Very Helpful
		1	2	3	4
e.	In general, from the client's perspective, how helpful have you been?	☐	☐	☐	☐

Part II - Barriers to the Working Relationship

There are many types of barriers to a good working relationship. The authority of the worker, for example, may make it difficult for a client to risk. Poor experiences with other professionals may cause a client to withhold trust. The worker may struggle with his or her own authority or bring a stereotype of the client to the engagement, based on past experiences. List the barriers in your relationship to this client:

1. _____

2. _____

3. _____

4. _____

5. _____

6. _____

Part III - Strategies for Strengthening the Working Relationship

Identify specific steps you will take to attempt to overcome barriers to an effective working relationship (e.g., raising the issue directly with the client; clarifying in your own mind the nature of your authority and under what conditions you are required to be a mandated reporter):

1. _____

2. _____

3. _____

4. _____

5. _____

6. _____

Student Self-Analysis of Stress and Support

This exercise is designed to aid social workers in identifying the nature of the stressors they experience as well as the sources of support available to them. Part I provides a simple stress inventory. Part II reviews the sources of support available to the worker and the potential obstacles that may block their use. Part III asks for the development of strategies for reducing stress and increasing support.

Part I - Worker Stress Assessment

In my opinion, my current job as a social worker is ...

		Strongly Agree	Agree	Uncertain	Disagree	Strongly Disagree
		1	2	3	4	5
a.	stressful	☐	☐	☐	☐	☐
b.	manageable	☐	☐	☐	☐	☐

In general, I find it particularly stressful to deal with the following clients and problems:

1. _____

2. _____

3. _____

4. _____

5. _____

6. _____

I believe the sources of my stress in dealing with these clients and problems are:

1. _____

2. _____

3. _____

4. _____

Part II - Worker Support Assessment

In general, when working on a difficult case . . .

		Strongly Agree	Agree	Uncertain	Disagree	Strongly Disagree
		1	2	3	4	5
a.	I seek consultation from my supervisor.	☐	☐	☐	☐	☐
b.	I seek consultation or help from my colleagues.	☐	☐	☐	☐	☐
c.	When offered help by other professionals with whom I work, I am receptive.	☐	☐	☐	☐	☐
d.	The support services that are needed to work on my case are available.	☐	☐	☐	☐	☐

Part III - Worker Strategies for Decreasing Stress and Increasing Support

Identify strategies that may help you cope with the identified stresses, given the available support systems.

1. _____

2. _____

3. _____

Appendix B

Standards and Expectations in Field Practice

Statements about expected student performance in the field on 24 core practice skills were developed by faculty and field instructors at the School of Social Work of the University of British Columbia. Under the direction of Dr. Kloh-Ann Amacher (1971), who was then coordinator of field instruction, a project was undertaken to describe these essential skills, to develop a rating instrument for the use of both students and field instructors, and to gather data that would provide a beginning statement of norms for each level of the undergraduate program.

This project was viewed as an initial step in the difficult task of developing tools for making more specific student assessments. The instrument described should be regarded as embryonic and in need of testing for reliability and validity. The normative data on the different program levels should also be considered preliminary. This material is shared as work in progress.

The approach taken required a lengthy process and considerable time and patience on the part of field instructors and students. First, a draft of descriptive statements about skills was circulated to methods instructors, and they were asked for feedback on its relevance, clarity, and inclusiveness. Instructors were also asked if the wording was sufficiently "theory free" and if the skills were applicable to work with individuals, families, small groups, and communities. Based on this feedback, the form was revised and distributed to field instructors and students to be used in midyear progress reports. The objective was to seek profiles and norms of actual performance at various points in the educational process.

The tentative instrument provides average, or mean, scores for each skill for students in the school's undergraduate programs. The undergraduate bachelor of social work (BSW) degree is viewed as the first professional degree level. Third-year students in this program have completed two years of general arts. They undertake a mixed program of social work and arts electives, which includes a supervised field practicum 2 days each week. Upon completion of the third year, they continue the fourth-year program, which consists of mostly social work courses with some arts electives. There is also a weekly two-and-one-half-day supervised field practicum. Upon completion of the fourth year, students are awarded a BSW degree.

The program for which scores are provided is the concentrated bachelor of social (CBSW) program. Students in this program have already obtained a bachelor's degree in some other area and have had a number of years of supervised social work or related experiences. The program consists of an extended school year (10 months) during which the students take their social work courses as well as a weekly two-and-one-half-day supervised field practicum. Upon completion of this program, students are awarded a BSW degree.

In presenting the material on the project to field instructors and students, the University of British Columbia acknowledged its interest in clear statements about expected performance in the field. The project's developers noted that, as educators, they "share the view that clarity about objectives can promote learning and increase equity in the evaluation of performance."

Detailed reports on the progress of each student on each of the skills were not expected. Rather, the material was presented for teaching and learning purposes, as a basis for discussion between students and field instructors, and to identify areas of particular strength or weakness for a student or a program.

Scoring Procedures

The skills were individually coded by field instructors in conferences with the student, according to the following:

(0)   The field instructor does not have evidence needed to make a judgment. The student may or may not have developed this skill. Not known.
(1)   The student has not yet developed this skill.
(2)   The student grasps the idea and is beginning to recognize in hindsight how it might have been applied in a given practice situation.
(3)   The student demonstrates the skill at a beginning level. Performance is uneven. Needs time and practice.
(4)   The skill is applied quite consistently, but there are gaps (e.g., not used with some clients, or some feelings are avoided, etc.).
(5)   The skill is an integrated part of the student's stance and style.

Average (mean) scores were computed for each class on each skill at midyear and the end of the year. Items coded "0" were excluded in the calculation. The average scores can be interpreted in terms of the coding sheet. For example, a 2.00 score would mean that the average student grasps the idea; a 2.50 would indicate that the average student grasps the idea and is beginning to demonstrate the skill in practice.

A total average on all skills also was computed for each group. The skills were ranked from highest level of achievement to lowest for the three groups combined, or the total BSW program.

Mean Scores on Core Skills

Overall average scores on all skills for all students in the three BSW groups at midyear and the end of the year were:

	Midyear Mean	End-of-Year Mean
Third-year BSW	2.24	3.28
Fourth-year BSW	3.70	4.53
CBSW (concentrated)	3.67	4.31

As these scores indicate, on the average, by midyear the third-year student was grasping the idea, seeing in hindsight what might have been done. Some students were beginning to apply some of the skills. Fourth-year and CBSW students were approaching a level of quite consistent application, with some gaps.

The following outline lists the core practice skills in rank order, from highest level of mastery to lowest, according to mean scores for the total group on each one.

1. *Ability to relate comfortably with clients who have different values or lifestyles, or who behave in ways that are labeled as "deviant" by the dominant society.*
   Students often struggle with value differences, at first not even recognizing their own values. Acceptance comes from self-awareness, understanding of the client, finding the areas of communality as well as difference, and respecting the client's right to be different.

	Midyear Mean	End-of-Year Mean
Third-year	2.88	3.56
Fourth-year	4.11	4.80
CBSW	4.23	4.61

2. *Ability to recognize the feelings in the client's expression.*
   This skill involves picking up and empathizing with expressed feelings, sensitivity to subtle or disguised expressions of feeling, perceptiveness about nonverbal clues, ability to tune in to probable feelings that are not quite expressed (e.g., the hurt beneath the anger), and perceptiveness about ambivalent feelings.

	Midyear Mean	End-of-Year Mean
Third-year	2.77	3.71
Fourth-year	4.00	4.63
CBSW	3.93	4.48

3. *Ability to clarify purposes, role, and agency function and to establish a mutual contract.*
   Initially, students may offer a solution without exploring the problem and the client's perception of needs. They may jump too quickly to provide a concrete service or have difficulty in explaining purpose or role without jargon. Eventually, they should develop a negotiating style, exploring the client's problems and wishes and explaining what the agency and worker can offer. Students should be able to make a tentative plan, consistently checking out, evaluating, and renegotiating the mutual understanding with the client of the goals and the process.

	Midyear Mean	End-of-Year Mean
Third-year	2.53	3.57
Fourth-year	3.89	4.81
CBSW	3.87	4.43

4. *Ability to recognize the range of factors that influence the client.*
   These factors may be biological (e.g., physical health); social (e.g., peer group pressures); psychological (e.g., vulnerability to separation); cultural (e.g., values); or political (e.g., legal recognition of rights). During the learning process, there can be a tendency to emphasize one of these aspects to the

exclusion of others. Students should develop a perceptiveness of all the aspects and an understanding of which factors are most relevant to a particular situation.

	Midyear Mean	End-of-Year Mean
Third-year	2.76	3.52
Fourth-year	3.80	4.81
CBSW	3.93	4.65

5. *Ability to tune in, relate differently, and use the self in different ways, according to the fluctuating needs of various clients at various times.*

    Initially, students succeed in establishing warm, positive relationships, then they begin to tune in more sensitively to the client's mood, become comfortable with quietness, join the client's moments of enthusiasm, and understand and accept the client's distorted images and feelings toward the worker without premature explanations or defensiveness. Students learn to empathize with that part of the client that resists change, as well as that part that strives for growth and begins to see that working relationships are based on understanding and a shared sense of purpose and need not always be warm and friendly.

	Midyear Mean	End-of-Year Mean
Third-year	2.43	3.52
Fourth-year	3.83	4.63
CBSW	3.83	4.30

6. *Ability to explore or to draw out facts or the story.*

    Students often begin by being hesitant and concerned about privacy and intrusion; they can be awkward about framing questions and fearful that the question might sound accusatory. They might not explore because they are uncertain about how to respond or use the information gained. With time, they should be able to offer support and explanation about the purpose of questions. They should also be able to clarify the communication, realizing that the message sent is not necessarily the message received.

	Midyear Mean	End-of-Year Mean
Third-year	2.28	3.52
Fourth-year	3.80	4.50
CBSW	4.00	4.35

7. *Ability to question and think critically about programs, theories, the effectiveness of interventions, alternative approaches.*

    This skill should be based on knowledge of policies, theories, and programs, and their history and rationales. Critical thinking should lead to ideas about changes and strategies to bring about change.

	Midyear Mean	End-of-Year Mean
Third-year	2.00	3.15
Fourth-year	4.05	4.13
CBSW	4.87	4.77

8. *Ability to move back and forth across the objectivity-subjectivity line.*
This skill involves the capacity to empathize with the client and the ability to step back and look objectively at the client, the self, and the interaction between them.

	Midyear Mean	End-of-Year Mean
Third-year	2.47	3.29
Fourth-year	3.84	4.50
CBSW	3.67	4.13

9. *Ability to formulate ideas about the process and the steps involved in moving from initial contracting through termination.*
Initially, students should question the purpose and the process and cannot be expected to have a clear view of what is helpful or why. They begin by seeing one useful step and move toward seeing a range of approaches.

	Midyear Mean	End-of-Year Mean
Third-year	2.45	3.33
Fourth-year	3.75	4.56
CBSW	3.80	4.30

10. *Ability to focus, maintain a sense of purpose and direction, and keep the client on the track.*
Students may show a beginning awkwardness or a need to be friendly and establish a relationship before getting down to business. They may be more comfortable in the role of friend. Eventually, they may begin to bring the discussion back to a focus—if the client is uncomfortable or avoiding the issues, they have some ability to discuss the client's discomfort. A consistent sense of purpose should emerge.

	Midyear Mean	End-of-Year Mean
Third-year	2.41	3.57
Fourth-year	3.85	4.63
CBSW	3.71	4.43

11. *Ability to integrate acceptance and expectation of clients.*
Students must learn to accept the client, then begin to make some demands, providing support along with the demands. Some students will go through periods of being too heavy on the acceptance side or too heavy on the demand side, eventually achieving the integration with some clients, possibly not with others. Eventually, they should develop a consistent style that incorporates both acceptance and expectation, with a sense of tact and appropriate timing.

	Midyear Mean	End-of-Year Mean
Third-year	2.52	3.29
Fourth-year	3.50	4.50
CBSW	3.80	4.23

12. *Ability to pick up themes, messages, and patterns underlying the client's presenting content.*

    Students begin to see in hindsight the relevance of the client's comments or digressions. They may wonder during interviews, Why is the client saying this to me *now*? Occasionally, they may comment on the themes and connections, as they learn to discern the messages that are embedded in other contexts. In group meetings, students begin to comment on the themes, helping members connect with one another.

	Midyear Mean	End-of-Year Mean
Third-year	2.34	3.24
Fourth-year	3.85	4.31
CBSW	3.50	4.19

13. *Awareness of feelings toward the client, ability to sort out the realistic from the provoked, and to identify self-generated responses to the client.*

    Awareness of one's own personal reactions can be a tool for understanding the client's interpersonal defenses. Students must first be aware of their feelings toward clients and then begin to question whether the feeling is realistic, part of the client's way of keeping distance, or if it stems from the worker's own unfinished business (e.g., an unrealistic need to mother, or resentment of domineering or ineffectual people).

	Midyear Mean	End-of-Year Mean
Third-year	1.96	2.89
Fourth-year	3.93	4.56
CBSW	3.64	4.09

14. *Ability to achieve an active-passive balance.*

    This skill combines passivity in letting the client struggle, and activity in the ability to speak up, suggest, advise, confront, or do for the client. Students may go through phases of being too active in giving suggestions, advice, or referrals and in doing for the client—or of being too passive, hesitant about making suggestions and giving opinions or information, but unwilling to do some things for some clients at some times. Eventually, they should be comfortable with both activity and passivity, and have a clear sense of the professional tasks.

	Midyear Mean	End-of-Year Mean
Third-year	2.38	3.25
Fourth-year	3.74	4.56
CBSW	3.60	4.04

15. *Ability to respond to feelings and facilitate their expression.*

    Early in their learning, students may tend to reassure clients prematurely or change the subject, because of their discomfort in experiencing too much of the client's pain, anger, or fearfulness or their uncertainty about how to respond. This moves toward the ability to express empathy, put unexpressed feelings into words, and explore both sides of ambivalence. The ability to accept and deal with hostility, to tolerate anxiety, and in group situations, to draw upon the cues or feelings of other group members also develops.

	Midyear Mean	End-of-Year Mean
Third-year	2.23	3.33
Fourth-year	3.53	4.31
CBSW	3.80	4.35

16. *Ability to respond to and accept both the rational and irrational components in the client's behavior.*

Students should relate to the rational components and learn to accept and not try to struggle against the inevitable irrational components by means of logic and debate. The irrational is purposive and rooted in fears and feelings that need to be addressed.

	Midyear Mean	End-of-Year Mean
Third-year	2.21	3.30
Fourth-year	3.59	4.63
CBSW	3.77	4.13

17. *Ability to understand, accept, and work with resistance.*

Some students will tend to give up when faced with resistance from a client; others will push, confront, exhort, advise, or battle with the client. Eventually, students should be able to discuss the client's resistance, the meaning to the client of being helped, and the fear and resentment inherent in change. They should recognize the need for defenses and for periodic avoidance of stressful content. Students should learn to respect the integrity of the human being. They should also learn to see how resistance reflects the client's efforts to maintain self-esteem and is a patterned approach to interpersonal relationships and social demands.

	Midyear Mean	End-of-Year Mean
Third-year	2.07	3.05
Fourth-year	3.71	4.63
CBSW	3.71	4.19

18. *Ability to share personal thoughts and feelings about the client and the client's situations.*

Students' inhibition can move to spontaneity, so feelings are conveyed bodily and verbally—awkwardly at first. At times, students will assume that the client would feel as they do without checking it out, or they will get into personal experiences that interrupt the flow and focus on the client's experience. This is followed by sensitivity to the client's reaction to their own feelings and the ability to sense when the client is embarrassed or fearful of the closeness, or simply resentful. Eventually, the student can discuss the relationship.

	Midyear Mean	End-of-Year Mean
Third-year	2.30	3.25
Fourth-year	3.63	4.50
CBSW	3.54	4.52

19.   *Ability to make referrals, help the client identify needs and resources, explore the client's feelings and expectations about the resources, and give clear information.*
Students should check out a resource and know about eligibility, the services actually provided, and the clientele served. They should be able to discuss the client's previous experiences and feelings about similar resources. Referrals should be based on a discussion of the client's hopes and motivation and personal priorities. There should be follow-through feedback from the client about the experience and its usefulness, clearing up misunderstandings.

	Midyear Mean	End-of-Year Mean
Third-year	2.08	3.45
Fourth-year	3.81	4.33
CBSW	3.42	4.55

20.   *Ability to accept the authority of the professional role and make difficult decisions, without abusing power and control over the client.*
Students can be very hesitant to use their authority, as in apprehending a child or in setting firm limits in situations in which the client is a danger to himself or others. There can also be a tendency to use power to punish when a client has been frustratingly uncooperative.

	Midyear Mean	End-of-Year Mean
Third-year	1.76	2.78
Fourth-year	3.43	4.54
CBSW	3.79	4.27

21.   *Ability to help the client select goals that maximize the client's motivation, capacity, and opportunity.*
Students may be too protective, not making demands. Or they may be too ambitious, imposing unreasonable expectations on the client, thinking only of long-range goals without being able to see the short-range, realizable steps toward longer term goals. Students should work in partnership with the client in establishing clear goals, articulating first steps, and achieving goals. They should have a sense of consistently helping the client to do his or her work, achieve his or her goals.

	Midyear Mean	End-of-Year Mean
Third-year	2.00	3.38
Fourth-year	3.47	4.44
CBSW	3.53	4.33

22.   *Ability to use programming, structures, and/or educative approaches.*
Over time, students will become selective about the clients who may benefit from these approaches and clear about the relationship of the approach to the client's needs and goals. They will be able to explain the purpose with clarity and get feedback.

	Midyear Mean	End-of-Year Mean
Third-year	1.92	3.18
Fourth-year	3.38	4.64
CBSW	3.50	4.20

23. *Ability to articulate aspects of the assumptions, theories, and knowledge base that shape the understanding and the action.*

    Students may be spontaneous and intuitive without understanding the "whys" and "hows." In the early stages, they often need directions and prescriptions but move toward greater independence in thinking things through for themselves. Initial efforts to apply theory in practice situations can be awkward and self-conscious. Eventually, the thinking process becomes integrated and natural and consistently guides the worker's activities without the loss of spontaneity, intuitiveness, and feeling.

	Midyear Mean	End-of-Year Mean
Third-year	1.93	3.05
Fourth-year	3.25	4.38
CBSW	3.21	4.23

24. *Ability to use research concepts in the analysis, planning, and evaluation of practice in routine work with any case, group, or community assignment.*

    This implies an appreciation of the relevance of research principles to practice, not just to empirical studies. This would include (a) knowledge of the range of possible data collection methods and the ability to make a well-reasoned selection of methods in a particular situation, (b) knowledge of the major types and sources of error in the social worker's use of data, (c) knowledge of and ability to use the criteria by which the adequacy of the data collected in practice situations may be assessed for its validity and usefulness in case planning, and (d) ability to evaluate evidence relevant to the effectiveness of the student's intervention.

	Midyear Mean	End-of-Year Mean
Third-year	1.06	1.33
Fourth-year	3.13	3.90
CBSW	2.33	3.44

Videotape Programs on Practice and Field Instruction

A number of teaching aids are available for optional use with the author's text *The Skills of Helping Individuals, Families and Groups* (3rd ed.). These programs are described in detail in this section.

Skills of Helping

A series of three programs in which Dr. Lawrence Shulman identifies and illustrates core practice skills for work with individuals, families and groups, as well as with other professionals. The three programs are: (1) Preliminary, Beginning and Work Phases, (2) Leading a First Group Session, and (3) Working With the System. The second program includes videotape excerpts from a first session of a married couples group led by Dr. Shulman. Discussion focuses on the core skills in the engagement phase of practice.

Dynamics and Skills of the Middle Phase of Practice

In this two-part series, Dr. Shulman and Dr. Alex Gitterman focus on the often overlooked middle phase of practice in a co-led workshop with six social work students. The programs are: (1) Focus and Direction With the Overwhelming Client and (2) Integrating the Personal With the Professional Self. Student practice examples are used to illustrate how to find a starting point with an overwhelmed family, work with a battered wife and a battering husband, integrate the worker's personal and professional self, as well as other issues.

Core Skills for Field Instructors

A series of five, color videotape programs in which Dr. Shulman identifies and illustrates core skills necessary for field instructors to work with practicum students.

The programs are organized according to the phases of work, with each program designed to help field instructors at a particular stage in the school year.

Program 1: Starting With the Student

A combination of presentation and discussion with agency field instructors at the start of the school year. Through the use of role play and detailed reconstruction of conversations with students, examples are explored of how to prepare for a student's arrival, deal with the initial student anxiety, and help the student settle in quickly in the agency. In addition, the skills of contracting with the student are examined, including clarifying purpose, clarifying role, reaching for feedback, and dealing with authority issues (e.g., grading).

Program 2: The Student and the Client

This program focuses on how a field instructor can help the student to develop the skills for tuning in to the client, responding directly to indirect client cues, and contracting with the client. The parallel process, in which the field instructor demonstrates the skills in working with a student that, in turn, the student needs to use with the client is discussed throughout the presentation. Also discussed are the issues of selecting appropriate assignments, when to have a student start working with clients, and how to be helpful after the first client interviews.

Program 3: Middle Phase of Field Instruction

This program is designed to be used in the middle part of the school year. It focuses on the problems of evaluation and of dealing with student defensiveness; helps students make a more effective use of the field instructor; presents the use of process or audiovisual recordings; and serves as an effective means for teaching in field instruction conferences.

Program 4: Student's Impact on the Agency System

This program focuses on how to help students deal with questions and concerns about agency policy and procedures that emerge during the course of the school year. It is based on the assumption that social workers have some responsibility for trying to constructively influence their own agency's delivery of service. This program thus teaches social work students how to assess their role in the system, develop informal and formal means for influencing policy or procedures, and effectively communicate with other staff. This is often a neglected, but important, area because field instructors must first have a sense of their own ability to influence their agency before they are able to help students develop a proactive attitude.

Program 5: Ending With the Student

This program examines the dynamics common to the ending phase of work with students, many of which are parallel to those of endings with clients. It discusses and illustrates ways in which the field instructor can end effectively with his or her student, thus modeling the ending skills, while at the same time helping the student develop the skills for effective endings with clients.

Videotape series are available for sale in the United States and for sale, rent, or preview in Canada from:

Instructional Communications Centre
McGill University
550 Sherbrooke Street West
Suite 400
Montreal, Quebec, Canada H3A 1B9
Telephone: (514) 398-7200
Fax: (514) 398-7339

Tapes are available *only* for rent or on-site preview:

Film/Video Rental Center
Syracuse University
1455 East Colvin Street
Syracuse, NY 13244-5150
Telephone: (800) 345-6797 or (315) 443-2452
Fax: (315) 443-9439

Appendix D

Recommended Readings

Abbott, A. A. (1986). The field placement contract: Its use in maintaining comparability between employment-related and traditional field placements. *Journal of Social Work Education, 22,* 57–66.

Abramson, J., & Fortune, A. E. (1990). Improving field instruction: An evaluation of a seminar for new field instructors. *Journal of Social Work Education, 26,* 273–286.

Alperin, D. E. (1989). Confidentiality in field placement. *Journal of Social Work Education, 25,* 98–108.

Austin, M. J., & Pecora, P. (1985). Evaluating supervisory training: The participant action plan approach. *Journal of Continuing Social Work Education, 3* (3), 8–13.

Bloom, M., & Fischer, J. (1982). *Evaluating practice: Guidelines for the accountable professional.* Englewood Cliffs, NJ: Prentice-Hall.

Bogo, M., & Vayda, E. (1987). *The practice of field instruction in social work.* Toronto: University of Toronto Press.

Doureck, H. J., & Kasper, B. (1990). Teaching practice evaluation to field instructors: A comparative study. *Journal of Teaching in Social Work, 4* (2), 105–125.

Drolen, C. (1991). Teaching undergraduate community practice: An experiential approach. *Journal of Teaching in Social Work, 5* (1), 35–47.

Ellison, M. L. (1991). *A study of effective and ineffective field instructor behavior.* Unpublished doctoral dissertation, University of North Carolina.

Fox, R., & Zischka, P. C. (1989). The field instruction contract: A paradigm for effective learning. *Journal of Teaching in Social Work, 3* (1), 103–116.

Freeman, E. M., & Brownstein, O. (1987). A process for teaching clinical practice. *The Clinical Supervisor, 5* (4), 59–77.

Gatz, Y., Thyer, B. A., Patten, S., & Parrish, R. (1990). Evaluating the effectiveness of field experience in a part-time, off-campus MSW program: The student's point of view. *Journal of Continuing Social Work Education, 5* (2), 11–14.

Gingerich, R. M., Jr. (1984). Generalizing single-case evaluation from classroom to practice setting. *Journal of Education for Social Work, 20,* 74–82.

Hartman, W. K. (1990). *The effect of evaluation on learning in graduate social work direct practice field instruction.* Unpublished doctoral dissertation, Rutgers University, New Brunswick.

Kapp, M. B. (1984). Supervising professional trainees: Legal implications for mental health institutions. *Hospital and Community Psychiatry, 35,* (2): 143–147.

Kissman, K., & Tran, T. V. (1990). Perceived quality of field placement education among graduate social work students. *Journal of Continuing Social Work Education, 5* (2), 27–31.

Koroloff, N. M., & Ryne, C. (1989). Assessing students' performance in field instruction. *Journal of Teaching in Social Work, 3* (2), 3–16.

Larsen, J., & Hepworth, D. H. (1982). Enhancing the effectiveness of practicum instruction: An empirical study. *Journal of Education for Social Work, 18,* 50–58.

Lazzari, M. M. (1991). Feminism, empowerment, and field education. *Affilia: Journal of Women and Social Work, 6* (4), 71–87.

Lewis, S. (1987). The role of self-awareness in social work supervision. *Australian Social Work, 40* (2), 19–24.

Limberger, J., & Marshack, E. (1988). *Educational assessment in the field: An opportunity for teacher-learner mutuality.* Presentation at the Annual Program Meeting of the Council on Social Work Education, Atlanta, GA.

Livingston, D., Davidson, K. W., & Marshack, E. F. (1989). Education for autonomous practice: A challenge for field instructors. *Journal of Independent Social Work, 4* (1), 69–82.

Lowy, L. (1983). Social work supervision: From models toward theory. *Journal of Education for Social Work, 19* (2), 55–62.

McRay, R. G., Freeman, E. M., & Logan, S. L. (1986). Cross-cultural field supervision: Implications for social work education. *Journal of Social Work Education, 22* (1), 50–56.

Munson, C. E. (1987). Field instruction in social work education. *Journal of Teaching in Social Work, 1* (1), 91–109.

Polinger, E. J. (1991). *The effect of student-field instructor similarity on their respective perceptions of the field practicum in social work education.* Unpublished doctoral dissertation, University of Maryland, Baltimore.

Raphael, F. B., & Rosenblum, A. F. (1989). The open expression of differences in the field practicum: Report of a Pilot Study. *Journal of Social Work Education, 25* (2), 109–116.

Rapp, C. A., Chamberlain, R., & Freeman, E. (1989). Practicum: New opportunities for training, research and service delivery. *Journal of Teaching in Social Work, 3* (1), 3–16.

Raskin, M., Skolnik, L., & Wayne, J. (1991). An international perspective of field instruction. *Journal of Social Work Education, 27,* 258–270.

Raskin, M. S. (Ed.). (1989). *Empirical studies in field instruction.* New York: Haworth Press.

Richan, W. C. (1989). Empowering students to empower others: A community-based field practicum. *Journal of Social Work Education, 25,* 276–283.

Rosenblum, A. F., & Raphael, F. B. (1991). Balancing students' right to privacy with the need for self-disclosure in field education. *Journal of Teaching in Social Work, 5* (1), 7–20.

Schneck, D., Grossman, B., & Glassman, U. (Eds.). (1990). *Field education in social work: Contemporary issues and trends.* Dubuque, IA: Kendall Hunt.

Sheafor, B. W., & Jenkins, L. E. (1982). *Quality field instruction in social work program development and maintenance.* New York: Longman.

Showers, N., & Cuzzi, L. (1991). What field instructors of social work students need from hospital field work programs. *Social Work in Health Care, 16* (1), 39–52.

Shulman, L. (1992). *Instructor's guide for the skills of helping.* Itasca, IL: F. E. Peacock.

Simons, R. L. (1987). The impact of training from empirically based practice. *Journal of Social Work Education, 23,* 24–30.

Smith, S. L., & Baker, D. R. (1989). The relationship between educational background of field instructor and the quality of supervision. In M. S. Raskin (Ed.), *Empirical studies in field instruction* (pp. 252–270). New York: Haworth Press.

Sowers-Hoag, K., & Thyer, B. (1985). Teaching social work practice: A review and analysis of empirical research. *Journal of Social Work Education, 21,* 5–15.

Thyer, B. A., Williams, M., Love, J. P., & Sowers-Hoag, K. M. (1989). The MSW supervisory requirement and field instruction: Does it make a difference? In M. S. Raskin (Ed.), *Empirical studies in field instruction* (pp. 249–256). New York: Haworth Press.

Wayne, J. (1988). A comparison of beliefs about student supervision between micro and macro practitioners. *The Clinical Supervisor, 6*(3/4), 271–279.

REFERENCES

Amacher, K. (1971). *Explorations into the dynamics of learning in field work.* Unpublished doctoral dissertation, Smith College, Northhampton, MA.

Arlow, J. A. (1963). The supervisory situation. *Journal of the American Psychoanalytic Association, 11*, 574–594.

Bulhan, H. A. (1988). *Frantz Fanon and the psychology of oppression.* New York: Plenum Press.

Dewey, J. (1916). *Democracy and education: An introduction to the philosophy of education.* New York: Free Press.

Doehrman, M. J. (1972). *Parallel processes in supervision and psychotherapy.* Unpublished doctoral dissertation, University of Michigan, Ann Arbor.

Galm, S. (1972). *Issues in welfare administration: Welfare—an administrative nightmare.* U.S. Congress, Subcommittee on Fiscal Policy of the Joint Economic Committee, Washington, DC: Government Printing Office.

Gondolfo, R., & Brown, R. (1987). Psychology intern ratings of actual and ideal supervision of psychotherapy. *Journal of Training and Practice in Professional Psychology, 1*, 15–20.

Heppner, P., & Roehlke, H. (1984). Difference among supervisees at different levels of training. *Journal of Counseling Psychology, 31*, 76–90.

Holt, J. (1969). *How children learn.* New York: Pitman.

Kadushin, A. (1973). *Supervisor-supervisee: A questionnaire study.* Madison: School of Social Work, University of Wisconsin.

Mayer, J. E., & Rosenblatt, A. (1975). Objectionable supervisory styles: Students' views. *Social Work, 20*, 184–189.

Olmstead, J. & Christenson, H. E. (1973). *Effects of agency work contexts: An intensive field study.* Report no 2. Washington, DC: U.S. Department of Health, Education, and Welfare, Social Rehabilitation Services.

Pincus, J. D. (1986). Communication, job satisfaction and job performance. *Human Communication Research, 12*, 395–419.

Schwartz, W. (1964, January). *The classroom teaching of social work with groups.* Paper presented at the Annual Program Meeting of the Council on Social Work Education, Toronto.

Schwartz, W. (1979, March). *Education in the classroom.* Paper presented at the Annual Program Meeting of the Council on Social Work Education, Boston.

Scott, W. R. (1969). Professional employees in the bureaucratic structure. In Etzioni Amitai (Ed.), *The semiprofessions and their organizations* (pp. 82–140). New York: Free Press.

Shulman, L. (1972). *Group work and effective college teaching.* Unpublished doctoral dissertation, Temple University, Philadelphia.

Shulman, L. (1978). A study of practice skill. *Social Work, 23*, 274–281.

Shulman, L. (1981). *Identifying, measuring, and teaching the helping skills.* New York: Council on Social Work Education and the Canadian Association of Schools of Social Work.

Shulman, L. (1991). *Interactional social work practice: Toward an empirical theory.* Itasca, IL: F. E. Peacock.

Shulman, L. (1992). *The skills of helping individuals, families and groups* (3rd ed.). Itasca, IL: F. E. Peacock.

Shulman, L. (1993). *Interactional supervision.* Washington, DC: National Association of Social Workers.

Shulman, L., Robinson, E., & Luckyj, A. (1981). *A study of supervision skills: Context, content, and process.* Unpublished report, School of Social Work, University of British Columbia, Vancouver.

Wilson, S. J. (1981). *Field instruction: Techniques for supervisors.* New York: Free Press.

Worthington, E. L., & Roehlke, H. (1979). Effective supervision as perceived by beginning counselors in training. *Journal of Counseling Psychology, 26,* 64–73.

Lawrence Shulman, MSW, EdD, is an educator, practitioner, social work researcher, and author of ten books on the subjects of social work practice and supervision.

Dr. Shulman graduated from Temple University in 1972 with an EdD in educational psychology and from Columbia University in 1961 with an MSW in social work practice. Since obtaining his doctorate, Dr. Shulman has taught in Canada at the School of Social Work at McGill University and at the University of British Columbia, and in the United States at the School of Social Work at Boston University, where he is currently professor and chair of the group work sequence.

His research on direct practice in public human services, as well as health care, has been commissioned by private foundations and by the government of Canada. Dr. Shulman has also provided consultation to U.S. state and city government and nonprofit organizations, to Canadian nonprofit organizations, and to the government of Hong Kong. In addition, he is used widely by many agencies, universities, and professional associations as a consultant and trainer in the areas of direct practice, field instruction, classroom teaching, child welfare, and supervision and administration.

In addition to publishing books and monographs and producing videotapes, Dr. Shulman also wrote the consultation entry in the 18th edition of the *Encyclopedia of Social Work* published by the National Association of Social Workers. He serves on the editorial boards of *Social Work with Groups*, *Journal of Teaching in Social Work*, *The Clinical Supervisor,* and *Groupwork.*

Dr. Shulman serves on the Program Planning and Faculty Development Commission of the Council on Social Work Education and is chair of the Commission on Group Work and Social Work Education of the Association for the Advancement of Social Work with Groups. He is also a member of the National Association of Social Workers, the American Association of University Professors, and the Bertha Reynolds Society.

Dr. Shulman has been a fundraiser for the Democratic National Committee, and during the last presidential campaign, founded and chaired Social Workers for Clinton '92. Currently, he serves on the reelection campaign committee for Democratic Senator Edward Kennedy of Massachusetts.